PRECIOUS
THOUGHTS

ABBEY OF GETHSEMANI
TRAPPIST, KENTUCKY

May 13 1962

Dear Jim,

Yesterday I received a very moving letter from the Stalling telling me about Everyman, & about his sailing today. I had also seen a copy of the Bulletin about it (it is on the novices notice board now.) Tried to reach him by telegram to say my prayers go with him. I am saying mass for the three in Everyman this morning, in about three hours from now. It is at present still early & dark & the birds are waking up.

There is something ominous about the title Operation Dominic. The AEC is identifying itself no doubt with the (Dominican) Inquisition. The final payoff will probably be called Operation Ignatius — the destruction of Europe & America.

I think the courage & alertness manifested in the building & sailing of Everyman is significant in a high degree. The CNVA is alive as few organizations are. This is the moment of Truth — or close to it. And yet the project is also inevitably very much of an improvisation. You must be careful of that, because the temptation to multiply improvisations as if they were miracles may be dangerous to the CNVA eventually. What you need is that Ashram, & deep roots from which these things grow more slowly & firmly. But one may say this is no time for anything to happen slowly.

God bless you all, with all my affection in xr
Tom

Please don't print this anyplace.

truth

PRECIOUS THOUGHTS

Daily readings from the correspondence of Thomas Merton

Selected and edited by
FIONA GARDNER

DARTON·LONGMAN+TODD

First published in 2011 by
Darton, Longman and Todd Ltd
1 Spencer Court
140-142 Wandsworth High Street
London SW18 4JJ

ISBN: 978-0-232-52883-1

A catalogue record for this book is available from the British Library.

Designed and typeset by Judy Linard
Printed and bound by Scandbook AB

CONTENTS

ACKNOWLEDGEMENTS

I would like to thank Dr Paul M. Pearson, Director and Archivist of The Thomas Merton Center, Bellarmine University, in Louisville, Kentucky, for his support and guidance. Also I am very grateful for the efforts of Anne McCormick and all the trustees of The Merton Legacy Trust in giving permission for the book and helping to establish contact with the publishers Farrar, Straus and Giroux who have kindly agreed to the use of these extracts.

As always thanks to Virginia Hearn at DLT for her professional and personal support. Finally, many thanks and appreciation to Peter Ellis, for his interest and help with proof reading the text.

Over the years my love for the writings of Thomas Merton has been nurtured and inspired by friends and colleagues both in The Thomas Merton Society of Great Britain and Ireland and in The International Thomas Merton Society, so this book is dedicated to them.

PREFACE

Thomas Merton, 'whose precious thoughts and dear bottomless letters enrich me and make me happy'. This is how Boris Pasternak described his correspondence with the monk and spiritual writer.[1]

Thomas Merton (1915–1968) was a Trappist monk based in the Abbey of Gethsemani, in Kentucky, North America. He was also a prolific writer, a poet and a prophet. He wrote about his childhood, adolescence and early adulthood, including his conversion to Christianity, in his autobiography *The Seven Storey Mountain*. Following the publicity surrounding this best-seller Merton began to receive a great deal of correspondence. It is estimated that Merton wrote over 10,000 letters to approximately 2,100 correspondents, though probably the actual number is higher.[2] Correspondents included many who sought spiritual advice and guidance from someone whom they recognised as having struggled to make sense of life and to find God. Some of Merton's correspondence is serious, extending over many years; some a single thoughtful reply to a spiritual concern; some funny or politically challenging.

There is no one type of person who wrote to Merton, the range is enormous and there is no limit to the subject matter covered. Some time ago selected letters were gathered into five volumes and the 'precious thoughts' included in this book have been taken from those collections, which are currently out of print. One of the skills of Merton as a communicator is that at times it can feel as if he is also communicating beyond the particular correspondent to a reader he has not known. The extracts chosen in this book are those that I believe speak to us still, although it is over forty years since Merton's death. In a sense spiritual searching belongs outside time and place, but when Merton raises spiritual concerns in the context of society it seems to have a deep resonance with contemporary life.

In this twenty-first century spiritual needs remain, although religion is for many something unfamiliar, irrelevant and apart from everyday life. God, if God exists, can feel too far away, and Christ and the lives of monastics and the saints seem to belong to another earlier and perhaps less knowing age. Religious practices and the living realities of those following Christ have little acknowledged significance now and are not part of mainstream thinking; they hardly enter most people's thoughts. The deeper aspects of life are largely missing or disconnected from the source, and there is no value or dignity in many lives which can feel disappointing or without meaning. Yet the spiritual searching carries on, and people search where they can for inspiration, nuggets of hope, fragments of faith, and wonder about the purpose of life. Merton understood this alienation, fragmentation, and disconnection, and spent his monastic life making connections with people, with nature, and in community.

Merton's inner search is for connection and realisation of what he calls the true self and for the gradual disconnection and detachment from the false self – the false self demanded by the world and that we use to hide from God and from the person that we are meant to be. The route to finding our true self, and thereby God, lies for Merton in silence and contemplation. This is a place where concepts and ideas are unimportant and if present can obscure the path. This is an acceptance that we cannot 'know', and that not knowing is a state of mind that has to be increasingly tolerated. This is surrendering to something that is more than our self. The extracts in this book mostly reflect these issues.

The daily readings selected here have been chosen because they offer an opening into something other – they are chosen to provide a way into both silence and contemplative prayer. They lead ultimately to God. I think this is what Pasternak meant when he wrote about Merton's letters as both 'dear' – both warm and invaluable, hinting at the pearl of great price that can be found within them – and 'bottomless' – there is no limit but rather a possibility of the infinite.

As one of his early correspondents wrote, 'Yes, your silence speaks well between the lines; and your words mean more than they seem to mean'.[3] The same wise correspondent offered Merton some advice in October 1941, two months before he decided to enter the monastery at Gethsemani, and some years before the publication of *The Seven Storey Mountain,*

> You have begun to go on that road that will eventually lead you to sell all to buy that pearl of great price.
> So, because of that, people are already coming to you. Take them simply, as you do, reverently, as you should, and lift them, and yourself thru them, ever higher and higher toward Him who has been lifted up to draw all things to Himself.[4]

The majority of the letters written by Merton appear steeped in this advice. He is straightforward with each correspondent, and yet respectful of whom they are and their circumstances in life, even if in disagreement with them he searches for a connection. Merton is present in his responses. The letters may sometimes appear muddled, contradictory or passionate but there is a clear sense of Merton speaking directly even urgently to the situation. Yet there is something more in that many of the letters especially those in response to correspondents seeking spiritual guidance are imbued by a light – there is something generous and precious given in Merton's reply. It is these precious thoughts that can be made available again, so there is another connection now made with us as the unknown recipients – the unknown readers.

One affect of reading these extracts, one at a time, day by day, over a year, is to gradually lift us towards divinity. As has been said, 'Our big commitments are lived out inch by inch, day in day out, and step by step... a succession of little things which anchor one's life more and more securely in God'.[5] Sometimes it's easier to take a small passage, and, rather than read it through as we might read a novel or newspaper, instead allow the passage to lead us deeper into the silence between the lines, and the deeper meaning that can be found in some of the words. Merton wrote that the contemplative has a special way of reading – rather than devouring the words they are savoured. Then the experience becomes one of spiritual feeding and nurture. Reading and meditating on certain words, and seeing what arises from the slow savouring, allow us to be open to experiential knowledge of God, to be inspired. Merton was a wonderful advocate of honouring the subjective experience of God, an experience he believed was open to anyone from any setting and from any background. He thought that the personal motive for reading should be to open oneself up to real contact with God. 'By reading I can give myself to God, give my mind to the light of His truth in order that I may serve Him with all the love of my heart'.[6]

The extracts have been chosen generally to fit with the seasons, and otherwise selected as words that seem to speak to all who are searching. Some of the selected extracts have been lightly edited. It is to be noted that Merton was writing before the change to inclusive language, and though it is highly likely that he would have used it the words are kept in their original form as requested by the Merton Legacy Trust. Similarly the use of capitalization has also been faithfully replicated which means it is not always consistent. The details of the recipient of the letter extract and where the full text can be found are placed at the end of the book. This is so that the experience for the contemporary reader is to the fore and thoughts about the actual recipient do not act as a diversion.

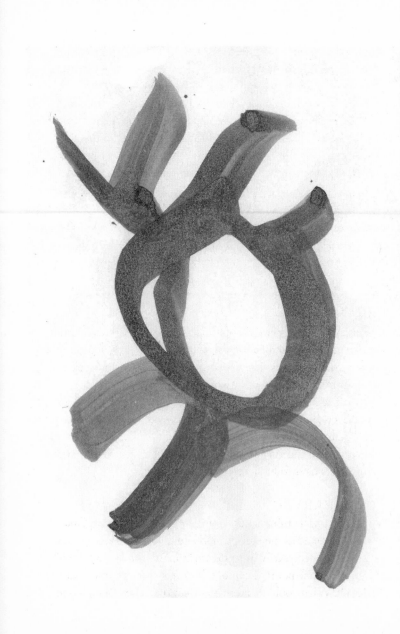

JANUARY

1 JANUARY

I can tell you that in reality life is good and a wonderful gift, and the more you put into it the better it is. But you must really grow up to be free, and truth loving, and sincere all the way with yourself and others. Don't live on illusions. You don't have to, reality is right there in front of you, and it is better than any illusion.

2 JANUARY

The concrete existential situation you are in here and now, whatever it is, contains for you God's will, reality. Your only job is to accept it as it is, because it is His will, and seek to fulfil it because it is the truth, not because it pleases you, gets you off a hook, or on a hook, or makes you feel safe, or whatever. But in order to do this you have to really believe deeply in God's love for you, and see that even the 'evil' in your life can serve the purposes of His love, now that it is over and the effects have to be suffered.

3 JANUARY

The great basic thing is remaining united by love with God's will considered as the pure ground and root of everything (not objectified necessarily in some anthropomorphic way). Here faith is the one point of contact. It brings one into immediate contact. What could be more real than that, even though one 'feels' nothing. The great thing is the purity and simplicity of our consent …

4 JANUARY

… I do not really have the feeling that we are searching for God by different ways. At root one searches for God by only one way, i.e. in following the truth with all the sincerity of one's conscience. Is it not a fact that we are on the same path after all? I feel myself to be very close to you. There are not two Gods – mine and yours. But we have all lived in different circumstances, and God alone sees our hearts. Who knows if he does not take more satisfaction in yours than in mine? These questions are meaningless because we do not know what he does with them …

5 JANUARY

There is that mysterious 'grace' of which the theologians speak not knowing of what they are speaking and of which clerics sometimes preach in a way that makes it suspect and odious to us. There is always this grace of God for which it suffices to seek, to ask for deep in one's heart. It is often given to us without our asking, without our knowing anything about it.

6 JANUARY

We must love the truth wherever it is found; we must go straight to the truth without wanting to glance backward and without caring about what school of theology it represents. The Church must truly be our Mother, which means that she must be the Church of the love of Christ; she must welcome us with a mother's love that shares her wisdom with us.

7 JANUARY

… Since the way we 'find' the Face of God is in faith, as long as we are in this mortal life, the basis of all interior prayer is faith. And the function of faith is to purify our hearts of all that is not faith, including all imaginings and desires that have nothing to do with God and His love. On the other hand, everything willed for us by God and everything related to His love can be material for prayer if it is used by faith to seek Him. Ordinarily however we must seek Him directly, as best we can, in our interior prayer. Meditation on His words will be a great help. Because in reflecting on His words with love and faith, we open our hearts to receive secret knowledge of Him together with an increase of love.

8 JANUARY

… Like every other Christian I am still occupied with the great affair of saving my sinful soul, in which grace and 'psychology' are sometimes in rather intense conflict. I am certainly aware of the fact that my life is not necessarily a history of fidelity to grace. Like every other Christian I can only admit my failures and beg the Lord to have mercy on me.

9 JANUARY

Now you ask about my method of meditation. Strictly speaking I have a very simple way of prayer. It is centred entirely on attention to the presence of God and to His will and His love. That is to say that it is centred on *faith* by which alone we can know the presence of God. One might say this gives my meditation the character described by the Prophet as 'being before God as if you saw Him'. Yet it does not mean imagining anything or conceiving a precise image of God, for to my mind this would be a kind of idolatry. On the contrary, it is a matter of adoring Him as invisible and infinitely beyond our comprehension, and realizing Him as all. My prayer tends very much toward what you call *fana*. There is in my heart this great thirst to recognize totally the nothingness of all that is not God.

10 JANUARY

I think too that we suffer (not the least I myself) from the disease of absolutes. Every answer has to be the right answer and, not only that, the final one. All problems have to be solved as of now. All uncertainties are intolerable. But what is life but uncertainties and a few plausible possibilities? Even the life of faith, in practice, is full of contingencies, and rightly so. That is why it is a life of faith. And its certainties are dark, not absolutely clear. Nor are they the kind we can use to produce immediate conviction in the interlocutor …

11 JANUARY

All I can say is that God will surely understand your good intentions as well as your weakness, and He is on your side. So have courage and don't give up. And don't waste energy hating yourself. You need that energy for better purposes …

12 JANUARY

… I am coming to realize that there is a subtle way in which the world grips us and will not set us free: for we must realize that the tyranny of worldly power today holds people precisely by continual anguish and torments them with insecurity, in order every day to get a little better grip. That is the demonic thing about this cold war and hot war and the ceaseless news … One must weep for the world, like Staretz Silouane, whom I love as you do. One must even, as he did, keep our souls in 'hell' without despairing. But also we must gradually get so that the world and its rule of terror does not reach in to try to dominate our inner soul.

13 JANUARY

There is nothing wrong with being subjective, and there is a time for it. The point is, however, not to get bogged down in it and examine too minutely what 'I feel' and why 'I' feel it. Because, after all, it is all pretty accidental.

14 JANUARY

Well, we won't really get out of the wilderness until everything is pressed out and there is nothing left but the pure wine to be offered to the Lord, transubstantiated into His Blood. Let us look forward to that day when we will be entirely in Him and He in us and the Father in and over all. Then there will be true peace which the world cannot give ...

15 JANUARY

Let us then continue united in prayer and faith, and realize more and more the truth and mercy of God in our lives. For we are called above all to be signs of His mercy in the world, and our fidelity will in its turn be a small sign to others of His fidelity, not that our fidelity has any value of itself, but it enables Him to give us richer blessings and to manifest Himself in doing good to us who are nothing.

16 JANUARY

The best my friendship can offer you is prayer, during the psalms at night, in my Mass at dawn. (I have a rare privilege, unappreciated and unthought of by almost all priests even here, of saying Mass just at sunrise, when the light of the sun falls on the altar, and powerfully lights up the mystery of the divine presence spoken of in so many, many prayers for 'illumination', like this morning's postcommunion: 'Come to meet us always O Lord with the heavenly Light everywhere, that we may discern with clear mind the mystery of which you have made us partakers, and that we may enter into it with awe and love'.)

17 JANUARY

My prayer is then a kind of praise rising up out of the centre of Nothing and Silence. If I am still present 'myself' this I recognise as an obstacle about which I can do nothing unless He Himself removes the obstacle. If He wills He can then make the Nothingness into a total clarity. If He does not will, then the Nothingness seems to itself to be an object and remains an obstacle. Such is my ordinary way of prayer, or meditation. It is not 'thinking about' anything, but a direct seeking of the Face of the Invisible, which cannot be found unless we become lost in Him who is Invisible.

18 JANUARY

I forget exactly what you are saying – something about the feminine: but it seems to me that the heart of the mystery of Israel is hidden motherhood, and that is the key to the dialogue between Israel and the Church – an impossible dialogue perhaps as long as we are all too far from our own inner reality (we = not you and me, but our groups). The Church should be the revelation and fulfilment of the Motherhood in Israel. No Father is involved but God and this is the great scandal to a community in which the Father is everything. But no matter, Father or Mother, what is important is the Child.

19 JANUARY

I agree with you about the constant sense of one's sinfulness, because we constantly assert ourselves, the delusion of ourselves, against the simplicity and truth of God. We cannot help it, this is our condition. Hence our life is a constant struggle with unreality, and the thing that complicates it is that the unreality in us is what seems to itself quite sincerely to be struggling for the truth. I do not really understand this at all. But the Bible is what seems to fit the situation best …

20 JANUARY
The air of the world is foul with lies, hypocrisy, falsity, and life is short, death approaches. We must devote ourselves with generosity and integrity to the real values: there is no time for falsity and compromise. But on the other hand we do not have to be greatly successful or even well known. It is enough for our integrity to be known to God. What we do that is pure in His sight will avail for the liberty, the enlightenment, and the salvation of His children everywhere.

21 JANUARY
Let us pray for one another to grow in hope and freedom and do so precisely in and by that anguish which is really a great good though we would certainly prefer any other at the time it is with us …

22 JANUARY
I believe that the only really valid thing that can be accomplished in the direction of world peace and unity at the moment is the preparation of the way by the formation of men who, isolated, perhaps not accepted or understood by any 'movement', are able to unite in themselves and experience in their own lives all that is best and most true in the various great spiritual traditions. Such men can become as it were 'sacraments' or signs of peace, at least. They can do much to open up the minds of their contemporaries to receive, in the future, new seeds of thought. Our task is one

of very remote preparation, a kind of arduous and unthanked pioneering.

23 JANUARY

First, it is true that one who is learning to meditate must also learn to get along without any support external to his own heart and the gifts of God. Hence it is good for such a one to have to remain in silence without reading or even using vocal prayers sometimes, in order to come to terms with the need for inner struggle and discipline. On the other hand this is not a universal rule. There are times when it is necessary to read, and even to read quite a lot, in order to store up material and get new perspectives.

24 JANUARY

Too often today the idea of 'hope' is presented in a totally untheological and secular form, as a kind of pious optimism that 'everything will be all right', presumably because it is just somehow the nature of things to be all right. But as we know, it is not exactly the nature of things to be all right, since man has a way of following his sinful will in strange directions, and causes have effects.

25 JANUARY

In the dark night through which we travel it is good to hear the voices of those who have not forgotten the Holy and Merciful God Who seeks to save us from ruin, Whose heart is set upon us as upon what is most precious to Him in His creation.

26 JANUARY

But besides the interior exigencies of the Spirit there are also hard external facts, and they too are 'God's will', but nevertheless they may mean that one is bound to a certain mediocrity and futility: that there is waste, and ineffective use of grace (bad way to talk, but you understand). The comfortable and respectable existence that you and I lead is in fact to a great degree *opposed* to the real demands of the Spirit in our lives. Yet paradoxically we are restricted and limited to this. Our acceptance of these restrictions cannot purely and simply be regarded as the ultimate obedience that is demanded of us. We cannot say that our bourgeois existence is purely and simply the 'will of God'. It both is and is not. Hence the burning and the darkness and the desperation we feel. The sense of untruth, of infidelity, even though we try as best we can to be faithful. … We are *held back* from the deep and total gift which is not altogether possible to make in a conventional and tame setting where we do not suffer the things that the poor and disinherited and the outcast must suffer. The crosses we may find or fabricate in this life of ours, may serve to salve our conscience a little, and legitimately so: but we are not in the fullest sense Christians because we have not fully and completely obeyed the Spirit of Christ.

27 JANUARY

As for spiritual life: what I object to about 'the Spiritual Life' is the fact that it is a part, a section, set off as if it were a whole. It is an aberration to set off our 'prayer' etc. from the rest of our existence, as if we were sometimes spiritual, sometimes not. As if we had to resign ourselves to feeling that the unspiritual moments were a dead loss. That is not right at all, and because it is an aberration, it causes an enormous amount of useless suffering.

Our 'life in the Spirit' is all-embracing, or should be. First it is the response of faith receiving the word of God, not only as a truth to be believed but as a gift of life to be lived in total submission and pure confidence. Then this implies fidelity and obedience, but a total fidelity and a total obedience. From the moment that I obey God in everything, where is my 'spiritual life'? It is gone out the window, there is no spiritual life, only God and His word and my total response.

28 JANUARY
… The mark of a contemporary holiness: this vision of the 'dark side' of wisdom, this hope that struggles with despair, this feeling of being in hell. This is the 'dark side' of the truth, the beauty of a wisdom which seems to be hidden in the chaotic disorder of sin. Oh, how discouraging it sometimes is to see what little good, true good, one is capable of. How false and disgusting so much conventional piety appears to be.

29 JANUARY
There is bound to be fruitfulness where there is real life.

30 JANUARY
Though the omnipresence of lies and of the Devil may frighten us, we must not surrender to tragedy. … It is not the lies we should see, but the truth with its darkened face, so like the Servant of the Lord who has no beauty, who is neither noble nor great, yet who comes forth like a shoot from the parched earth. And at the same time it is the Beauty of God who is always playing in the world before the Face of the Father.

31 JANUARY
… In the presence of the darkness, the cloud of falsity and pretence, of confusion, of evasion, of desecration, one grows

more and more to distrust words, to distrust even human communication itself. There grows in my heart a need to express something inexpressible, and I do not dare to find out what it might possibly be. So I can only fall back on half-articulate utterances. Forgive the lack of meaning.

FEBRUARY

1 FEBRUARY

You have a concrete situation to face and accept as positively and constructively as possible. That is just about all you have to do, but it may be hard work to do it consistently. The basic principle is that you must stop wasting time blaming yourself for things which can no longer be helped and probably could not be helped at the time either. And you must accept the results of the past: your karma, let's call it. And you must go on from where you are, and try to go only where you can realistically go. And if on top of it your machinery stops functioning properly, well, that is just part of the situation you have to accept and work with. Eventually you will come through and figure out why, etc. Or you will see in some way what it is about. If you can't see now, don't panic, you will later.

2 FEBRUARY

… Let us keep one another in our prayers and may the Lord watch over us, for without Him we are nothing, not even dust and not even smoke. In the light of that, the mere fact we are 'here' ought to be an encouragement but sometimes it isn't. The capacity to be distracted turns out to be a blessing.

3 FEBRUARY

Your intuition that Christ suffers in us in the Dark Night of the Soul seems to me to be especially apt and true. In the Night of Sense it is we who suffer in our own emptiness; in the Night of the Spirit he is emptiness in us, *exinanivit semetipsum*. The special awfulness of that seeming void can certainly be taken as a personal presence, but without duality, without too much of the subject-object relationship. But above that.

Everybody is suffering emptiness. All that is familiar to us is being threatened and taken away... there may be little or nothing left and we may all have evaporated. Surely one cannot feel comfortable or at ease in such a world. We are under sentence of death, an extinction without remembrance or memorial, and we cling to life and to the present. This causes bitterness and anguish. Christ will cure us of this clinging and then we will be free and joyful, even in the night.

4 FEBRUARY

... Stop hurting yourself. Be at peace. Realize God's love and mercy and your own freedom ...

5 FEBRUARY

It is all much simpler than we think: we always want to make the spiritual life something added on to the rest of life, and so to speak *compensating* for our normal life. What compensation is needed? Our normal life is life 'in Christ'.

6 FEBRUARY

To me the Buddhist discipline of meditation and asceticism are very interesting because of the very sure psychological realism they display. I believe that the wisdom of these techniques is not sufficiently appreciated. It is a pity that

Christian scholars tend to approach Buddhism with many illusions, believing it to be in some sense a 'rival religion'. To think this is, in many ways, a complete misunderstanding. The very essence of Buddhism is that it is 'non-competitive' because it does not set up barriers and divisions, but rather destroys them, seeking the deepest unity, beyond all oppositions, and seeking it on a philosophical and ascetic plane, rather than by means that would conflict with the Christian sacraments, necessarily. We are dealing with different levels and different ways of approaching the ultimate unity.

7 FEBRUARY

… You may have a great deal to suffer, but if you accept it realistically and without too much fear, with real trust in Him, it will do great things for you. But it may be quite painful and confusing. …

This business of believing in God's love for you not as an abstraction but as a reality, as *the* reality, is very important.

8 FEBRUARY

… God was seemingly never more absent from the world and yet His Christ, the Word, is walking about all around us all over the face of the earth, and in a terrible hour …

9 FEBRUARY

… We must seek Him and not ourselves. That is to say we must not seek some special experience or 'state' but only God, and accept whatever He may will for us. In our prayer we should avoid everything that makes us uselessly examine and analyse ourselves, and simply go to Him in faith, even if it means that we have to be very patient with a form of prayer that seems dark and arid. He will teach us if we are patient and trust in Him.

10 FEBRUARY

The basic principle for authentic interior prayer (I do not like the term 'mental' prayer because it suggests that it is all in the 'mind') is the same as the basis for the monastic life itself: *si revera Deum quaerit* [does the novice truly seek God]. Our interior prayer is simply the most intimate and personal way in which we seek the Face of God.

11 FEBRUARY

Really we have to pray for a total and profound change in the mentality of the whole world. What we have known in the past as Christian penance is not a deep enough concept if it does not comprehend the special problems and dangers of the present age. Hairshirts will not do the trick, though there is no harm in mortifying the flesh. But vastly more important is the complete change of heart and the totally new outlook on the world of man. We have to see our duty to mankind as a whole. We must not fail in this duty which God is imposing on us with His own hand.

12 FEBRUARY

Yes, Lent is a joy. And we do not have to be worried about relishing the cleanness of it. It feels better not to be stuffed. A little emptiness does one good ...

13 FEBRUARY

And so we turn our eyes to the great feast of Christian hope: the Resurrection. ... The real root of Christian hope is the presence of the Risen Lord among us and in us by His Spirit which is the Spirit and power of love. The power of the Resurrection is the power of love that is stronger than death and evil, and its promise is the promise that the power of this love is ours if we freely accept it. To accept it is not just a matter of making a wish, but of entire and total commitment to the Law of Christ which is the Law of Love.

14 FEBRUARY

Perseverance – yes, more and more one sees that it is the great thing. But there is a thing that must not be overlooked. Perseverance is not hanging on to some course which we have set our minds to, and refusing to let go. It is not even a matter of getting a bulldog grip on the faith and not letting the devil pry us loose from it – though many of the saints made it look that way. Really, there is something lacking in such a hope as that. Hope is a greater scandal than we think. I am coming to think that God (may He be praised in His great mystery) loves and helps best those who are so beat and have so much nothing when they come to die that it is almost as if they had persevered in nothing but had gradually lost everything, piece by piece, until there was nothing left but God. Hence perseverance is not hanging on but letting go.

15 FEBRUARY

Yes, it is true that our love for God easily falls into tepidity and aridity when we do not come unceasingly back to the knowledge of His love for us. In truth, it is His love which is at the same time the cause and the term of our loving knowledge of Him. It is His love that invites us to find Him everywhere, in the Scripture, in nature, in our own hearts, in our duties – and I add my own voice: in solitude!

16 FEBRUARY

… About being united with God's will: I don't mean that you should specially formulate this in words frequently but rather just develop a habitual awareness and conviction that you are completely in His hands and His love is taking care of you in everything, that you need have no special worries about anything, past present or future, as long as you are sincerely trying to do what He seems to ask of you. And of course by that I mean simply what is called for by the obvious needs of the moment, duties of state, people you meet, events to cope with, sicknesses, mistakes, and so on. 'When hungry eat, when tired sleep'. It is basically the same attitude as the Zenists', and presupposes that one has been able to let go of useless preoccupations with oneself. And with too clear a concept of God, too, for that matter.

17 FEBRUARY

At every turn, we get back to the big question, which is the question of the person as void and not as individual or empirical ego. I know of no one in the West who has treated of person in such a way as to make clear that what is most ourselves is what is least ourself, or better the other way round. It is the void that is our personality, and not our individuality that seems to be concrete and defined and present etc. It is what is seemingly not present, the void, that is really I. And the 'I' that seems to be I is really a void. But the West is so used to identifying the person with the individual and the deeper self with the empirical self ... that the basic truth is never seen. It is the Not-I that is most of all the I in each one of us. But we are completely enslaved by the illusory I that is not I, and never can be I, except in a purely fictional and social sense. ... There is only the Void which is I, covered over by an apparent I. And when the apparent I is seen to be void it no longer needs to be rejected, *for it is I*. How wonderful it is to be alive in such a world of craziness and simplicity ...

18 FEBRUARY

I would not be *thinking about* God's love, but just have a habitual awareness of this fact, that whether you think about it or not, everything will be taken care of, and hence what I really mean by it is not thinking about yourself and not trying to figure everything out.

19 FEBRUARY

… The important thing is who are you: you are not a 'man with a problem', or a person trying to figure something out… you are you and that is the important thing. For, you see, when 'I' enter into a dialogue with 'you' and each of us knows who is speaking, it turns out that we are both Christ. This, being seen in a very simple and 'natural' light, is the beginning and almost the fullness of everything. Everything is in it somewhere. But it makes most sense in the light of Mass and the Eucharist.

20 FEBRUARY

Certainly the greatest danger today is to assume that we have to accept society and its ills as a divinely given and final reality to which our thinking must be adjusted, without any attempt to change anything according to deeper standards. That way, we just let 'society' push us along, and we forget that we are society. That if we do not strive to build and guide society according to reason and to conscious principles, then it will lead us and sink us by the power of our own unconscious forces, with a little help from the devil.

21 FEBRUARY

And then this: do not depend on the hope of results. When you are doing the sort of work you have taken on, essentially an apostolic work, you may have to face the fact that your work will be apparently worthless and even achieve no result at all, if not perhaps results opposite to what you expect. As you get used to this idea you start more and more to concentrate not on the results but on the value, the rightness, the truth of the work itself. And there too a great deal has to be gone through, as gradually you struggle less and less for an idea and more and more for specific people. The range tends to narrow down, but it gets much more real. In the end, as you yourself mention in passing, it is the reality of personal relationships that saves everything.

22 FEBRUARY

God's absence among religious people, among religious groups, His absence where it is claimed that He is worshipped, is something terrifying today. Or sad in the utter extreme, because it is not His wrath, exactly, it is His loneliness, His lostness among us. That He waits among us unknown and silent, patiently, for the moment when we will finally destroy Him utterly in His image … And leave Him alone again in the empty cosmos.

23 FEBRUARY

… Do not be discouraged. The Holy Spirit is not asleep. Nor let yourself get too frustrated. There is no use getting mad at the Church and her representatives. First there is the problem of communication, which is impossible. Then there is the fact that God writes straight on crooked lines anyway, all the time, all the time. The lines are crooked enough by now. And we I suppose are what He is writing with, though we can't see what is being written. And what He writes is not for peace of soul, that is sure …

24 FEBRUARY

… This awful mistake of the West, which is certainly not a 'Christian' mistake at all, but the fruit of Western aggression, was the idea that one had to 'convert' the East and make it change in every way into a replica of the West. This is one of the great spiritual crimes of man in its own unconscious way and we are only beginning to reap the fruit of it in China, the Congo, etc.

25 FEBRUARY

… I feel more and more the paradox and mystery of my vocation, such as it is. This is my place and yet I have never felt so strongly that I have 'no place' as I have felt here since becoming fully reconciled to this as 'my place'. My place is in reality no place, and I hesitate to act as if I were anything but a stranger anywhere, but especially here. I am an alien and a transient, and this is the last happiness that is possible to me: but a very real one. More real than all the others I thought I knew before it. Everything is alien to me and I am alien to everything, even contemplation, even writing.

26 FEBRUARY

In meditation, the less conscious you are of performing some special 'exercise' the better off you will be. If a book helps you to keep relaxed and free and un-self-conscious, then it is a good thing. However, don't just read all the time. The purpose of meditation is to get us in contact with Jesus. It is like making a phone call. When you have got the person you want to talk to, you don't hang up immediately and then ring up all over again. Sometimes the line is busy, however. Then you ring again. Only make sure that the line is not busy at your end when He is trying to reach you …

27 FEBRUARY

There comes a time when it is no longer important to prove one's point, but simply to live, to surrender to God and to love.

28 FEBRUARY

The real hope, then, is not in something we think we can do, but in God who is making something good out of it in some way we cannot see. If we can do His will, we will be helping in this process. But we will not necessarily know all about it beforehand.

29 FEBRUARY

So the next step in the process is for you to see that your own thinking about what you are doing is crucially important. You are probably striving to build yourself an identity in your work and your witness. You are using it so to speak to protect yourself against nothingness, annihilation. That is not the right use of your work. All the good that you will do will come not from you but from the fact that you have allowed yourself, in the obedience of faith, to be used by God's love. Think of this more and gradually you will be free from the need to prove yourself, and you can be more open to the power that will work through you without your knowing it.

MARCH

1 MARCH

Let us be united in prayer that we may truly grow in faith and breadth of vision, and be able to accept anything that comes. There are reasons behind all that goes on in the world, and we do not always see them. May God give us light, faith and strength to go forward in His love …

2 MARCH

Well, I plough through things and seem to come out all the time anyway. I am really very happy that in all this wrestling with myself, I am really getting rid of an awful lot of Merton, but the void that replaces him is a bit disconcerting: except that I know God is there. One thing is sure: I do not particularly want the survival of the person and even the writer I have been. Although I do have enough sense to realize that this is what I shall always probably be. But my true self is not one that has to be thought about and propped up with rationalizations. He only has to be lived, and he is lived, in Christ, under the surface of the unquiet sea in which the other one is busy drowning.

3 MARCH

The chief problem is that of freedom of the spirit, and allowing the Christian to develop and grow, rather than keeping him in a straitjacket forever. On the other hand, of course, so many people *desire* control and though they do not even admit this, they fear freedom and want to be told what to do all the time, provided that they can sometimes have the pleasure of resisting and attracting the attention of authority. And of criticizing others who do not absolutely conform.

4 MARCH
In the long run, the basic thing is faith and prayer however one may look at it, because without these there is no real love: love does not have deep enough roots without them. If one has a deeper and hidden stability in these things, then the externals can change as much as you like.

5 MARCH
And this loving care for natural creatures becomes, in some sense, a warrant of ... theological mission and ministry ... . I refuse in practice to accept any theory or method of contemplation that simply divides soul against body, interior against exterior, and then tries to transcend itself by pushing creatures out into the dark. What dark? As soon as the split is made, the dark is abysmal in everything, and the only way to get back into the light is to be once again a normal human being who likes to smell the flowers and look at girls if they are around, and who likes the clouds, etc. ... The contemplative life ... is simply the restoration of man, in Christ, to the state in which he was originally intended to live. ... To be living the life of the new creation in which the right relation to all the rest of God's creatures is fully restored.

6 MARCH
The suffering Servant is One: Christ, Israel. There is one wedding and one wedding feast, not two or five or six. There

is one bride. There is one mystery, and the mystery of Israel and of the Church is ultimately to be revealed as One. As one great scandal maybe to a lot of people on both sides who have better things to do than come to the wedding.

7 MARCH

However, we have to start from where we are, and respond to grace as we are, within our own communities and we have to take one step at a time. The main thing is to be ready to refuse nothing when the call really comes, and to be open to each little thing, each new opportunity to make our life more real and less of a systematic and mechanical routine. But we have to be patient and not demand instant sweeping results.

8 MARCH

One of the things I love about my life, and therefore one of the reasons why I would not change it for anything, is the fact that I live in the woods and according to a tempo of sun and moon and season in which it is naturally easy and possible to walk in God's light, so to speak, in and through his creation. … I seldom have to fuss with any such thing as 'recollecting myself' and all that rot. All you do is breathe, and look around. And wash dishes, type, etc. Or just listen to the birds.

9 MARCH

Not one of us can just pick up and walk out and from then on live the Sermon on the Mount literally: yet we should want to try as much as we can to live in that spirit. There is no question that the Christian spirit is truly a spirit of non-violence and love, and Christians who support a war like the one in Vietnam are no doubt in good faith, but they are far from realizing what they are really doing, or what the war really means.

10 MARCH

So the growth of population, the incidence of cancer, the splitting of the atom and chain reactions, the infinite noise of meaningless communication, so-called affluence in the big countries, and a thousand other symptoms all express the same thing, what it is we do not know because we are it. But we are swelling up in a strange spiritual and a-spiritual ferment and God alone knows what will come of it.

11 MARCH

Let us all pray for one another that we may give Our Lord what He asks of us, as best we can, and each will do a little toward the renewal of the whole Body.

12 MARCH

You are right in feeling a little fear at the greatness of the task, and the possible difficulties. You will certainly meet great difficulties, and heartbreaking opposition and disappointment in many ways. You may in fact even be deprived of tasting the full fruit of success. But if you simply forget about the results and do the work with all your heart because it is pleasing to God and for the benefit of your brothers, and if you take that as reward enough in this life, you will achieve far more than you could ever hope ...

13 MARCH

Basically our first duty today is to human truth in its existential reality, and this sooner or later brings us into confrontation with system and power which seek to overwhelm truth for the sake of particular interests, perhaps rationalized as ideals. Sooner or later this human duty presents itself in a form of crisis that cannot be evaded. At such a time it is very good, almost essential, to have at one's side others with a similar determination, and one can then be guided by a common inspiration and a communion in truth. Here true strength can be found. A completely isolated witness is much more difficult and dangerous. In the end that too may become necessary. But in any case we know that our only ultimate strength is in the Lord and in His Spirit, and faith must make us depend entirely on His will and providence. One must then truly be detached and free in order not to be held and impeded by anything secondary or irrelevant. Which is another way of saying that poverty also is our strength.

14 MARCH

I have my own way to walk, and for some reason or other Zen is right in the middle of it wherever I go. So there it is, with all its beautiful purposelessness, and it has become very familiar to me though I do not know 'what it is'. Or even if it is an 'it'. Not to be foolish and multiply words, I'll say simply that it seems to me that Zen is the very atmosphere of the Gospels, and the Gospels are bursting with it. It is the proper climate for any monk, no matter what kind of monk he may be. If I could not breathe Zen I would probably die of spiritual asphyxiation. But I still don't know what it is. No matter. I don't know what the air is either.

15 MARCH

Be patient and follow the way of simplicity with which God has blessed you. But things cannot help sometimes being filled with anguish, for all of us who seek to love Christ. Life is never in any way as simple as it ought to be: there are so many conflicts, not between good people and bad only but between the good and the good. This is worse, and produces unending confusion. We must seek peace in the underlying simplicity which is beyond conflict: and here we seek the naked presence of God in apparent nothingness. If only we find Him, the emptiness becomes perfectly full, and the contradictions vanish. But in order to do this we must be faithful to a will that is inscrutable, which does not reveal itself in simple and clear-cut decisions as we would like to think. Rather than try to find all the nuances of meaning and morality in each case, we must seize hold desperately on the first available indication and trust in God for all the rest.

16 MARCH

For the voice of God must always come to us at every moment both from near and far and from the point that is nowhere and everywhere, from the O of admiration which is a boundless circle, and from the humility of love that breaks through limits set by national pride and the arrogance of wealth and power. Let us then live in a communion which undermines the power and arrogance of the great of this world, which seeks to separate men in the power struggle.

17 MARCH

You can say absolutely nothing about the Church that can shock me. If I stay with the Church it is out of a disillusioned love, and with a realization that I myself could not be happy outside, though I have no guarantee of being happy inside either. In effect, my 'happiness' does not depend on any institution or any establishment. As for you, you are part of my 'Church' of friends who are in many ways more important to me than the institution.

18 MARCH

… For different reasons we are prisoners of grace in one way or another. And I suppose we can both say 'it is good for us to be here'.

19 MARCH

And this condition of mere humanity does not require solitude in the country, it can be and should be realized anywhere. This is just my way of doing it. What would seem to others to be the final step into total alienation seems to me to be the beginning of the resolution of all alienation and the preparation for a real return without masks and without defences into the world ...

20 MARCH

May God protect all those dear people who have so much to suffer and have such great need.

21 MARCH

Your nature is getting a bit rocked, and there is not much you can do about it. Do not attach too much importance to any individual happening or reaction, and do not look for very special significances: all is part of a purification process, with which you must be patient. You have an ego which you obviously cannot get rid of by ego-willing, and the more you try the more you will be in a bind. You cannot scheme, you cannot figure, you cannot worm your way out of it. Only God can unlock the whole business from the inside, and when He does, then everything will be simple and plain.

22 MARCH

Any question about unjust and useless suffering is difficult to answer, and I must admit that I do not have ready answers to such questions at hand. In the end, I believe the trouble comes from some imperfect way in which we imagine God 'willing' or 'permitting' these things, as if He were somehow a human being and outside of everything. Who knows? If human suffering has value, it is only from the fact that Christ, God

Himself, suffers it in us and with us. Who is to say that He does not in some way Himself suffer in the animals what they suffer? That is a possible answer. God cannot simply look on 'objectively' while His creatures suffer. To imagine Him doing so is to imagine something quite other than God.

23 MARCH

Ultimately, I think it is on this level that all our decisions have to be made today. What does God ask of ME?

So I pray that you may see what God is asking of you, really and truly, and that he may give you the strength to do just that, as best you can.

24 MARCH

What you say about the fact that you (and all of us) are unbelieving and that it is God in you who believes, is quite true. We do not realize how little faith we have, and the more people talk about 'my' faith, the more I wonder if they have it. … I have no idea what you may be in the eyes of God, and that is what counts. I do think, though, that you and I are one in Christ …

25 MARCH

Obviously the human element complicates everything but what else are we? Human, that's all. Dying is no answer either, but of course it is attractive since it promises liberation from all the ego jazz, emotions, etc. But what are you now, except what you are then?

26 MARCH

The first thing to be said, of course, is that Hagia Sophia is God Himself. God is not only a Father but a Mother. He is both at the same time, and it is the 'feminine aspect' or 'feminine principle' in the divinity that is the Hagia Sophia. But of course as soon as you say this the whole thing becomes misleading: a division of an 'abstract' divinity into two abstract principles. Nevertheless, to ignore this distinction is to lose touch with the fullness of God. This is a very ancient intuition of reality which goes back to the oldest Oriental thought. ... For the 'masculine-feminine' relationship is basic in *all* reality – simply because all reality mirrors the reality of God.

27 MARCH

Actually, life and death do not matter much and they are not our business to determine. The only thing we have to do is to seek in every way not to place any obstacle in the way of God's will that comes up inscrutably out of the Ground of our lives (this does not mean being totally weedless either).

28 MARCH

I have a deeper and deeper sense of the great importance of the Mass, as you too intimate in your letter. There is no question of it ...

29 MARCH

I would therefore accept the difficulties of your present situation as God's will, make a heroic gift of yourself, and accept all that He wants. If then He wants something else for you, He will certainly know how to bring it about. Do not be discouraged. He loves you very much. If you were the only person in the world, and needed Him to do so, He would descend to earth again and die for you. How then can you fear that He will abandon you? Trust in Him and repay His love with your whole heart ...

30 MARCH

It is true that we do not know where we are.

That there are circles within circles, and that if we choose we can let loose in the circle of paradise the very wrath of God: this is said by Boehme in his confessions. We are trying to bear him out, but children can, if they still will, give us the lie and show us our folly. But we are now more and more persistent in refusing to see any such thing. All we will see is the image, the image, the absurd image, the mask over our own emptiness.

31 MARCH

Nasrudin is about to fall in a pond, and a friend grabs him in time so that he does not fall in. Then his friend keeps reminding him, day after day, of the fact that he kept him from falling into the pond. Nasrudin finally loses patience, drags the friend down to the pond and then jumps in. 'Now', he says, 'will you finally leave me alone?'

Another: Nasrudin walks into a shop. The shopkeeper comes out and says: 'Can I help you?' N. says 'Have you ever seen me before?' 'No', says the shopkeeper. 'Then', says Nasrudin, 'how can you help me: how do you know it's ME?'

... The stories all have implications for Sufism and the mystical life.

APRIL

1 APRIL

Love can also be tough and uncompromising in its fidelity to its own highest principles. Let us be united in joy, peace and prayer this Easter and always. 'Fear not' says Jesus 'It is I. I am with you all days!'

2 APRIL

And so here we are in the middle of the mystery of the Passion. Our Lord has certainly had to do it all by Himself. We have not been much help to Him, ever, and perhaps we cannot be. And now with this tremendous destructive power, and with our incapacity to handle it, and our inability to think straight, and our best efforts going astray: it would be sad and discouraging, if we did not remember that the Cross itself is the sign of victory. But victory is one thing and 'success', in the dimensions familiar to us, is quite another. You are so right about prayer being the main thing: it is the realm that cannot be closed to us and cannot be got at. There we are strongest because we are frankly centred in our helplessness and in His power, not obsessed with fictions and trivialities …

3 APRIL

If we are dedicated to the mystery of Gethsemani, it means to say that we are in particular to be mindful of the Blessed Virgin's solitude and sorrow of heart in her compassion for the suffering of Christ in the Garden of Gethsemani where He was abandoned by all who loved Him and was betrayed by one of His disciples. I think then that this means our life as monks is lived especially under the sign of a kind of inner solitude and dereliction, and I know from experience that this is true. But in this solitude and dereliction we are united with others who are alone and solitary and poor.

4 APRIL

… God bless you … this Holy Week. I will be keeping you in my Easter Masses and ask the Lord to give you every blessing and joy and to keep ever fresh and young your 'child's mind' which is the only one worth having. May He grant us (as you so well say) to be both inebriated and sober in Christ, Confucians and Taoists. It is all-important for us to *be* in Christ what the great sages cried out to God for. May our studies help us to live what they hoped for, and may we be able to bring to the Orient hope and light, which by right is theirs: for Christ rose up in the East, and we sing to Him *'O Oriens'* in Advent. His is what William of St.-Thierry called the *orientale lumen*. To that great light let us be humbly devoted and let us seek its tranquil purity in which all lights are fulfilled.

5 APRIL

There is no joy but in the victory of Christ over death in us: and all love that is valid has something of that victory. But the power of love cannot 'win' in us if we insist on opposing it with something else to which we can cling, on which we trust because we ourselves can manipulate it. It all depends who is in control: our own ego, or Christ. We must learn to surrender our ego-mastery to His mastery. … Easter celebrates the victory of love over everything. *Amor vincit omnia.*

6 APRIL

... Life is on our side. The silence and the Cross of which we know are forces that cannot be defeated. In silence and suffering, in the heartbreaking effort to be honest in the midst of dishonesty (most of all our *own* dishonesty), in all these is victory. It is Christ in us who drives us through darkness to a light of which we have no conception and which can only be found by passing through apparent despair. Everything has to be tested. All relationships have to be tried. All loyalties have to pass through fire. Much has to be lost. Much in us has to be killed, even much that is best in us. But Victory is certain. The Resurrection is the only light, and with that light there is no error.

7 APRIL

Yet I feel, and I am sure you do, that we are really completely in God's hands and that, with all our incapacity, we can serve Him very well by staying there and responding to what our times ask of us, insofar as we can. If only He will give us the grace of lucidity and strength in all the diabolical confusion of the world – a confusion in which we share. How deeply we are involved in what we condemn.

8 APRIL

To be a flexible instrument in the hand of God is a great and sometimes terrible vocation. ... We are all in someway instruments. And we all have to be virtuosos at taking a back seat when necessary, way back. The prayer life of a flexible instrument cannot be well ordered. It has to be terribly free. And utterly responsive to a darkly, dimly understood command.

9 APRIL

... My life is in many ways simple, but it is also a mystery which I do not attempt to really understand, as though I were led by the hand in a night where I see nothing, but can fully depend on the Love and Protection of Him Who guides me.

10 APRIL

The Church is Christ, often a wounded and bleeding Christ, surely more often bleeding than glorious, in this age of history. Let us be very careful and faithful about avoiding everything that makes the wounds of division bleed more. I think that is going to be a very crucial point to keep in mind in the next few years. And let us meanwhile all pray for one another that we may be faithful and strong.

11 APRIL

In the last seven years I have found out somewhat of what God wants to do with people, and what His love means. When I say this life is wonderful it doesn't mean that every other vocation isn't wonderful too: but to be in the sort of place where God wants one: that is certainly a marvellous thing. As soon as you get set in your groove, boy do things happen!

12 APRIL

My best suggestion is that if the thought of God bugs her, she should forget it. It is not that necessary to be thinking about Him. We act as if He depended on our thoughts. And then of course we get involved precisely with a God that does not exist because He depends on us thinking about Him. Surely that's a waste of time. He can take very good care of us when we are not thinking about Him.

To put it another way: if there were no God whatever, I myself would still be living exactly as I live now and doing what I am doing. If that is the case, surely the 'question of the existence of God' is not all that important, is it? ... Words aren't going to do much at this point. If a person can accept her utter loneliness and realize it not as a lack or an impoverishment, but as a fullness and a ground of all freedom, then she can break through. But it may hurt …

13 APRIL
The religion of our time, to be authentic, needs to be the kind that escapes practically all religious definition. … One's whole being must be an act for which there can be found no word. This is the primary meaning of faith. On this basis, other dimensions of belief can be made credible. Otherwise not. My whole being must be a yes and an amen and an exclamation that is not heard. Only after that is there any point in exclamations and even after that there is no point in exclamations. One's acts must be part of the same silent exclamation. … If only they could realize that nothing *has to be* uttered.

14 APRIL
It is natural for you to feel terribly lonely and upset. Death is a terrible thing, and people cover it up with words so as to make it less terrible. But when you come face to face with it, there is nothing you can do or say. It is final. That is why you feel so lost about it. But yet, our faith tells us, it is not final in God's eyes. For man, it is the end. For man in Christ, it is just the beginning. If faith does not give us much comfort sometimes, that is to be expected. Faith is not just there for our comfort. It is there to make us grow, and reach out. You will find help when you get a little stronger and can help others a bit. Meanwhile, you must accept loneliness until our Lord teaches you what to do with it.

I will keep you in my prayers. Have courage. Ask Our Lord to bring you a deep understanding of His sorrow. That is how you will begin to understand your own sorrow.

15 APRIL

But Christ Himself is in us as unknown and unseen. We follow Him, we find Him ... and then He must vanish and we must go along without Him at our side. Why? Because He is even closer than that. *He is ourself.*

16 APRIL

Respect life, truth, growth, meaning, in yourself and in others, and you are not amoral.

17 APRIL

In Christ the world and the whole cosmos has been created anew (which means to say restored to its original perfection and beyond that made divine, totally transfigured). The whole world has risen in Christ, say the Fathers. If God is 'all in all', then everything is in fact paradise, because it is filled with the glory and presence of God, and nothing is any more separated from God. ...We are in paradise, and once we break free from the false image, we find ourselves what we are: and we are 'in Christ'.

18 APRIL

... We in the West are ready to talk about things like Zen and about a hundred and one other things besides, but we are not so eager to do the things that Zen implies: and that is what really counts. At the moment, I occasionally meet my own kind of Zen master, in passing, and for a brief moment. For example, the other day a bluebird sitting on a fence post suddenly took off after a wasp, dived for it, missed, and instantly returned to the same position on the fence post as if nothing had ever happened. A brief, split-second lesson in Zen. ... But the gist of it would be that the birds never stop to say 'I missed' because, in fact, whether they catch the wasp, or not, they never miss, and neither does Zen. We in the West are the ones with the hit-or-miss outlook on life, and so we hit and we miss. And in both cases the results are likely to be tragic. I fear our successes more than our failures.

19 APRIL
We underestimate St. Paul. We do not realize what a liberation he went through and how carefree and undetermined a Christian really should be, with no care save to listen to the Holy Spirit and follow wherever He beckons!

20 APRIL
We cannot get too deep into the mystery of our oneness in Christ. It is so deep as to be unthinkable and yet a little thought about it doesn't hurt. But it doesn't help too much either. The thing is that we are not united in a *thought* of Christ or a desire of Christ, but in His Spirit. ... I don't know if my letter about our oneness in Christ was clear. The other day a good distinction came to mind: but there is all the difference in the world between theology as *experienced* (which is basically identical in all who know and love Christ, at least in its root) and theology as *formulated* in which there can be great differences. In the former, it is the One Spirit who teaches and enlightens us. In the second it is the Church ...

21 APRIL
Thus what one 'sees' in prayer before an ikon is not an external representation of a historical person, but an interior presence in light, which is the glory of the transfigured Christ, the experience of which is transmitted in faith from generation to generation of those who have 'seen', from the Apostles on down. ... So when I say that my Christ is the Christ of the

ikons, I mean that he is reached not through any scientific study but through direct faith and the mediation of the liturgy, art, worship, prayer, theology of light, etc. ... Christ not as object of seeing or study, but Christ as centre in whom and by whom one is illuminated.

22 APRIL

... We too easily tend to focus our eyes on our sinfulness and nothingness and then we forget that we have risen with Christ, that we have a wonderful new life to live in His Holy Spirit, that we have been overwhelmed with His gifts. It is true that we do not appreciate them enough: but the best way to appreciate them more is to look at them, and look at God's love, instead of constantly looking at our own failures. If we wish to please God truly by our religious life, we must see that it is really a *life* and not just a living death ...

23 APRIL

I suppose what makes me most glad is that we all recognize each other in this metaphysical space of silence and happiness, and get some sense, for a moment, that we are full of paradise without knowing it ...

24 APRIL

You say you have a sense of bearing the sufferings of others. We all do. There is great sin in this country, and some people have to bear it. It is Christ who alone can give us strength to do this well, with love. We cannot afford to be just passive and negative. We have to try to make things better, by love, by awareness, by helping people to remedy their lot. I wish I knew definitely what needs to be done in each case. But these are the general principles. God bless you.

25 APRIL

As to your own desolation and loneliness: what can anyone say? It is the desolation of all of us in the presence of death and nothingness, but Christ in us bears it for us: without our being consoled. To accept non-consolation is to mysteriously help others who have more than they can bear.

26 APRIL

We must never forget that Christianity came to the west from the Orient. It is not purely and simply the 'religion of the west'. The specifically western elements which have come to be identified with Christianity are rather cultural and social elements, the outer garments of the religion, not the religion itself. Christianity, as Dr. John C. H. Wu, of China, has so well observed, is 'beyond East and West'. Christ is the fulfilment of the latent desires and aspirations of all religions and all philosophies. One must transcend them all to come to Him: yet in Him one finds all that was good and true in every other religion.

27 APRIL

The situation in this country grows darker and more tragic, so that I think even the most insensitive must begin to realize that there is something radically wrong. What is wrong is the indifference to God and to authentic religious and moral values, even among those who call themselves Christians – who are sometimes the worst in regard to things like racism, injustice, intolerance, hatred. At no time was it more evident that prayer and repentance were necessary here. ...

Never was a real renewal of the contemplative and monastic life more necessary.

28 APRIL

Let us certainly be united in prayer in these days of change. … May the Holy Spirit guide us all in making changes that will effect a genuine renewal, and not simply let us plunge madly into the latest fashions which are sometimes quite superficial …

29 APRIL

The reality of silence and solitude are of course essential. But it should be in a kind of dialectic with charity and help to your neighbours there. In other words, the help you give should clearly proceed from a love that is nourished by silence and prayer; it should manifest a compassion that is rooted in an intimate awareness of the sufferings of Christ. The fact that you will see Him suffering concretely in the poor there ought to help your contemplative prayer to be deeper and more real.

30 APRIL

After all, the great thing in life is to share the best one has, no matter how poor it may be. The sharing gives it value.

MAY

1 MAY

Identify with the Ground and you won't worry too much about the weeds. The Ground doesn't. And the Ground can't be anything but Good. In Himself He plants His own seeds without you knowing or being able to do much about it. Just don't go cultivating weeds on purpose, with the idea that they are something very special, either specially good or specially bad.

2 MAY

As for continual prayer. ... What is really meant of course is continual openness to God, attentiveness, listening, disposability, etc. In the terms of Zen, it is not awareness *of* but simple awareness. So that if one deliberately cultivates a distinct consciousness *of* anything, any object, one tends to frustrate one's objectives – or God's objectives. If one just thinks of it in terms of loving God all the time in whatever way is most spontaneous and simple, then perhaps the error can be avoided.

3 MAY

You complain of being idle. I feel as if I were too busy. It depends what you mean by idle & busy. One thing is true: you don't need to *accomplish* anything in order to please God, and He doesn't need anybody's movement & activity. But He does want your love and my love … I hope you will one day get settled in something you will know is definitely God's will and all directed to Him alone. Because that is the necessary thing.

4 MAY

My own part is to accept things as God gives them to me, and to enter into the confusion without too many illusions and too many hopes of making sense out of it all. I will try to diminish the evil and the hatred where I can, and I will try to bring light into the confusion when I am capable of doing so …

5 MAY

In any event, there is only one meeting place for all religions, and it is paradise. How nice to be there and wander about looking at the flowers. Or being the flowers.

6 MAY

To my mind, the Christian doctrine of grace (however understood – I mean here the gift of God's Life to us) seems to me to fulfil a most important function in all this. The realization, the finding of ourselves in Christ and hence in paradise, has a special character from the fact that this is all a free gift from God… the breakthrough of the realization that a sacrament, for instance, is a finger pointing to the completely spontaneous Gift of Himself to us on the part of God – beyond and above images, outside of every idea, every law, every right or wrong, everything high or low, everything spiritual or material. Whether we are good or bad, wise or foolish, there is always this sudden irruption, this breakthrough of God's freedom into our life, turning the whole thing upside down so that it comes out, contrary to all expectation, right side up. This is grace, this is salvation this is Christianity.

7 MAY

May we all grow in grace and peace, and not neglect the silence that is printed in the centre of our being. It will not fail us. It is more than silence. Jesus spoke of the spring of living water, you remember …

8 MAY

Speaking in monastic terms, of fidelity to the truth, to the light that is in us from God, that is the horror: everyone has been more or less unfaithful, and those who have seemed to be faithful have been so partially, in a way that sanctified greater evasions (the Grand Inquisitor). Perhaps the great reality of our time is this, that no one is capable of this fidelity, and all have failed in it, and that there is no hope to be looked for in any one of us. But God is faithful. It is what the Holy Week liturgy tells of His 'treading the winepress by Himself'. This, I think, is the central reality.

9 MAY

To me the 'light' of Christ in the ikons is simply a special case of the light which has now penetrated *everything*. …

Hence my Christ is the 'apophatic' Christ – light that is not light, and not confinable within any known category of light, and not communicable in any light that is not not-light: yet in all things, in their ground, not by nature but by gift, grace, death and resurrection.

10 MAY

I am still so dazed that I have not remembered half the things I forgot to say, or I would say some of them here. But of course they were never meant to be said, I suppose. They have been uttered in the Word and we can understand them all in His silence. Once a Zen master reproved a disciple saying: 'You are all right, except that you talk about Zen.' Yet of course they would immediately agree that an agreement *not* to talk about it would not be Zen either.

11 MAY
People still accuse me of being enthusiastic, but I guess I am a little saner than I used to be? Anyway it is good to be quiet enough to let God work and not get too much in His way with one's own pep, because when my own steam obscures everything things don't move nearly as fast.

12 MAY
I think you will especially like this passage [from Philoxenus] which discusses the *simplicity* which is a prime essential of spiritual life, and which was 'normal' to Adam and Eve in paradise. Hence it is a description of the 'paradise life' of prajna and emptiness.

Here is what he says. After saying that God was with them and 'showed them everything': 'They received no thought about Him into their spirit. They never asked: Where does He live, who shows us these things? How long has He existed? If He created all, was He Himself created? By whom? And we, why has He created us? Why has He placed us in this paradise? Why has He given us this law? All these things were far from their minds, because simplicity does not think such thoughts. Simplicity is completely absorbed in listening to what it hears. All its thought is mingled with the word of him who speaks. It is like the little child, completely absorbed in the person speaking to it'.

13 MAY

What you are looking for is Jesus, and He is hidden. You are not just looking for an interesting life with Him: you are looking for Him. To find Him is to be hidden, even from oneself.

14 MAY

The great consolation that no one can take away from us is that we are Christians, that we have died with Christ and risen with Him and are free ... and that we not only have 'privileges' which permit us to get away with little things here and there, through loopholes in the law – we are *obliged* by our Christian calling to be 'no longer under the Law'.

15 MAY

It is not easy to try to say what I know I cannot say. I do really have the feeling that you have all understood and shared quite perfectly. That you have seen something that I see to be most precious – and most available too. The reality that is present to us and in us: call it Being, call it Atman, call it Pneuma ... or Silence. And the simple fact that by being attentive, by learning to listen (or recovering the natural capacity to listen which cannot be learned any more than breathing), we can find ourself engulfed in such happiness that it cannot be explained: the happiness of being at one with everything in that hidden ground of Love for which there can be no explanations.

16 MAY

But the active side of Christianity is nothing without the hidden, passive and contemplative aspect. Indeed, without the secret, interior, lowly, obscure knowledge of God in contemplation, the activity of the apostle is empty and fruitless. Indeed, it is perhaps because the contemplative aspect of Christianity has been to a great extent ignored by so many in the west, that

Christianity has been less fruitful than it might have been in the east. It is the union with God in a darkness where nothing is seen or understood, that is the source of the mysterious love which is the life blood of Christianity. It is in the darkness of faith that the soul is united to Christ, and in this darkness the Holy Spirit, like an inexhaustible spring of living water, irrigates the dry wastes of the soul that is exhausted by attachment to the things of sense. This living water revives the soul and makes it capable of a love and compassion which are the most powerful of all spiritual forces because they are the power of God Himself in us: and God is Love.

17 MAY

All people are funny because they are at the same time real and false, and that is what is so good about it. Original sin is serious enough for it to be blasphemy to find a joke in it, and yet since from the first a Redeemer was promised, and since He is sent, and is in the midst of us, the mixture of reality and serious falsity that is everywhere becomes very funny if we see that in the midst of everything is the Christ, the Real One, Who does not mind our caricatures as much as we would if we were in His exact position. He sees it all in another way, through the lens of a mercy which does the same thing to everything as does Zen to whatever it looks at. (Zen can only do things to what it looks at for, of course, it redeems nothing.)

18 MAY

The great thing is not things but God Himself Who is not things but ourselves, and the world, and everything, lost in Him Who so fully IS that we come closer to Him by imagining He is not. The Being of all and my own Being is a vast emptiness containing nothing: I have but to swim in it and be carried away in it to see that this nothing is All. This too may be a distracting way of putting it: but everything is really very simple and do not let yourselves be disturbed by appearances of complication and multiplicity. *Omnia in omnibus Christus.* Let His Spirit carry you where He wills ...

19 MAY

The only advice I can give you is to seek God with sincere faith and concentrate on the essentials: His redemptive and merciful love to all.... His goodness to you in particular, the indications of His will for you as shown in your own life, the grace of Baptism you have received, by which Christ dwells in your heart, and the fact that you have received the Holy Spirit, the Spirit of Love, which helps you to understand and love others in spite of their faults and limitations, in spite of the harm they may do to you. These are the realities of the Christian life and the Church will fit into this pattern if you seek first the Kingdom of God and can stand on your own feet.

20 MAY

Those who have too many programmes and answers are absolutely blind and their ignorance leads them to destruction. Those who know that they do not know, are able at least to see something of what is in front of their nose. They can see a shadow of it, anyway. And they can move with the light and the shadow and keep from getting immediate sunstroke. So we must all move, even with motionless movement, even if we do not see clearly. A few little flames, yes. You can't grasp them, but anyway look at them obliquely. To look too directly at anything is to see something else because we force it to submit to the impertinence of our preconceptions. After a while though everything will speak to us if we let it and do not demand that it say what we dictate.

21 MAY

I want very much to say a loud 'No' to missiles and polaris submarines and everything which sneaks up on a city to destroy it, no matter whose city, no matter what the supposed wickedness of it. Who is to judge cities if not even Christ came to judge the world? For the just there is probably no pardon. If you know what I mean by 'just' – of course, unjust. That is one of the principal lessons of the Gospels: that the just are unjust and that those who are 'justified' are so only by mercy received and given, for it is this that brings them 'in line', for the line is mercy, not justice.

22 MAY

There is such a sea of wonderful things for you both to fall into and swim in – where can you begin? What are you reading, or doing, or thinking? ... Best of all is to go to the sources, the Fathers, the Bible, and I am sure you do ...

23 MAY

Jesus leaves us on this earth long enough to learn that although this life seems drab, it is already heaven. And being in heaven does not mean escaping from our own poor limitations and littleness: it means learning to find heaven with our own littleness. Jesus emptied Himself in order to teach us this. We do not have to be great but simply to be ourselves – the selves whom He loved. ... The closer we come to God, the more we begin to be the person we have always been.

24 MAY

I see more and more the awful complexity of the Western mind, which is my mind also, for better or for worse. I have been meditating here and there on Buddhist classics, in a small way, and find there an admirable therapy and simplification, wonderfully adapted to clear the way for grace, provided one does not become obsessed with a pride in one's own skill in meditating (not necessarily an urgent danger for me) or one's interior purity (still less, I am afraid). If Buddhism is humble, then it can be wonderfully, admirably humble and can offer for the humility of Christ a beautiful and appropriate dwelling.

25 MAY
Because when somebody is right, then someone else is wrong, and this gets us forgetting that we are all wrong, or, in some sense, right. The thing is to see that unless we know we are wrong we cannot be right, because the only thing we can successfully be right about is the fact that we are all wrong. The one incontrovertible fact of human life. When one starts from that one, however, the rest begins to make sense.

26 MAY
Thus in the end I must do what everyone else does and fall back on the mercy of God and try, as far as I can, not to fail Him in His loving will for me. Certainly if I tried to please everyone, I would fail Him, and if I am to please Him I must inevitably displease a lot of very earnest and well-meaning people. And I intend to continue doing this without scruple.

27 MAY
The beauty of all creation is a reflection of Sophia living and hidden in creation. But it is only our reflection. And the misleading thing about beauty, created beauty, is that we expect Sophia to be simply a more intense and more perfect and more brilliant, unspoiled, spiritual revelation of the same beauty. Whereas to arrive at her beauty we must pass through an apparent negation of created beauty, and to reach her light we

must realize that in comparison with created light it is a darkness. But this is only because created beauty and light are ugliness and darkness compared with her. Again the whole thing is in the question of mercy, which cuts across the divisions and passes beyond every philosophical and religious ideal. For Sophia is not an ideal, not an abstraction, but the highest reality, and the highest reality must manifest herself to us not only in power but also in poverty, otherwise we never see it. Sophia is the Lady Poverty to whom St Francis was married. And of course she dwelt with the Desert Fathers in their solitude, for it was she who brought them there and she whom they knew there. It was with her that they conversed all the time in their silence.

28 MAY

There is everywhere a kind of hunger for the grace and light of the Spirit in forms that can be actually *experienced* … I have always tended more toward a deepening of faith in solitude, a 'desert' and 'wilderness' existence in which one does not seek special experiences. But I concur with these others in being unable to remain satisfied with a formal and exterior kind of religion … we need a real deepening of life in every area …

29 MAY

… Let us in any case have great love for Truth and open our hearts to the Spirit of God our Lord and Father, Compassion-ate and Merciful. He alone is Real, and we have our reality only as a gift from Him at every moment.

30 MAY

Not much point in longing for solitude, it is not something you get but something you have. It is you. What are you looking for? To see yourself as a happy object? It is a waste of time. Being solitary, I no longer give it a thought, because solitude is an illusion like everything else. The only ground is emptiness, which is love. And this is not something we generate under nice and favourable conditions. The conditions are unimportant. You know all this but I might as well say it.

31 MAY

The key to the whole thing is, of course, *mercy* and *love*. In the sense that God is Love, is Mercy, is Humility, is Hiddenness, He shows Himself to us within ourselves as our own poverty, our own nothingness (which Christ took upon Himself, ordained for this by the Incarnation in the womb of the Virgin) … and if we receive the humility of God into our hearts, we become able to accept and embrace and love this very poverty, which is Himself and His Sophia. And then the darkness of Wisdom becomes to us inexpressible light. We pass through the centre of our own nothingness into the light of God.

JUNE

1 JUNE

Love's debts have this in them that they are too great to be paid, and that therefore one loves to remain in debt. ... for this is what it is to be a Christian: simply to be Christ and not to realize it. In this there is nothing but reasons for humility, because everybody is Christ. But not everybody is able to work out, in his life, the meaning of who he is. Most people manage to obscure it and even deface it, sad to say. If this bewilders you, that is fine. It should. Anybody who understands such things has not understood.

2 JUNE

We do not see the way that lies ahead of us. It seems dark, but God is the Master of all destinies and His will is love. Let us then put aside everything else and trust ourselves completely to Him, giving ourselves to His love, and asking Him to enlighten us and guide us in the way of positive action if any such action is feasible. For the rest, we must have great patience and sustained fidelity to His will and to our ideals.

3 JUNE

It is most important that we pray for peace, and detach ourselves more and more from the futile and lying values of the world of men who are moving towards war carried by the momentum of enormous sins and lies. ... Society ... particularly in the west, is burdened by a history of infidelity and crime that are enormous, and all we do is excuse and palliate our falsity, trying to blame someone else who is as guilty as we are. We are all guilty, but that means that we must in a very special way avoid the final guilt of violence or of despair.

4 JUNE

I can no longer see the ultimate meaning of a ... life in terms of either 'being a poet' or 'being a contemplative' or even in a certain sense 'being a saint' (although that is the only thing to be). It must be something much more immediate than that. I – and every other person in the world – *must* say: 'I have my own special, peculiar destiny which no one else ever has had or ever will have. There exists for me a particular goal, a fulfilment which must be all my own – nobody else's – & it does not really identify that destiny to put it under some category – 'poet', 'monk', 'hermit'. Because my own individual destiny is a meeting, an encounter with God that He has destined for me alone. His glory in me will be to receive from me something He can never receive from anyone else – because it is a gift of His to me which He has never given to anyone else & never will. My whole life is only that – to establish that particular constant with God which is the one He has planned for my eternity!

5 JUNE

Total corruption. Everything is corrupt and corruption spreads from one structure to the other, although they all have more than enough. The only incorrupt things are silence, not knowing, not going, not waiting etc., mostly not saying. You are right that as soon as one has finished saying something it is no longer true. Heraclitus. Love is all right as long as statements are not made and as long as it does not itself become a programme, because then it is another tyranny.

6 JUNE
Now I enjoy the quiet of the woods and the song of birds and the presence of the Lord in silence. Here is Nameless Tao, revealed as Jesus, the brightness of the hidden Father, our joy and our life ...

7 JUNE
As for Providence: certainly I think the glib clichés that are made about the will of God are enough to make anyone lose ... faith. Such clichés are still possible in America but I don't see how they can still survive in Europe, at least for anyone who has seen a concentration camp. For my part, I have given up my compulsive need to answer such questions neatly. It is safer and cleaner to remain inarticulate, and does more honour to God. I think the reason why we cannot see Providence at work in our world is that it is much too simple. ... Actually it is God Himself who is in the concentration camp. That is, of course, it is Christ. Not in the collective sense, but especially in the defilement and destruction of each individual soul, there is the renewal of the Crucifixion. ... he *is* Christ. ... Insofar as we are Christ, we are our own Providence.

8 JUNE
It remains for you to trust God, not to make you infallible but to protect you from serious error and to make good the smaller mistakes. And thus with confidence in His guidance, even though you may not always interpret it correctly, you can advance peacefully. I am sure He will guide you safely in everything if you take care to keep your heart quiet and pure,

as best you can, and listen to His voice in simplicity, trying to avoid the more obvious illusions, and keeping as close as possible to the solid bedrock of faith. With that, He will do all the rest. And He will put books into your hands that will tell you what your friends cannot.

9 JUNE

The crisis of the world is, for one thing, a crisis of falsity. The enormous lies by which we live have reached a point of such obvious contradiction with the truth that everything is contradiction and absurdity. But I think it can be said, at least I feel that this is worth saying: woman has been 'used' shamelessly in our commercial society, and in this 'misuse' has been deeply involved in falsity. Think, for instance, of advertising, in which woman is constantly used as bait. And along with that, the mentality that is created for woman, and forced on her complacently, by the commercial world. She becomes herself a commodity. In a way the symbol of all commodities. In the false image of woman, life itself is turned into a commodity in its very source.

10 JUNE

I believe sometimes that God is sick of the rich people and the powerful and wise... of the world and that He is going to look elsewhere and find the underprivileged, those who are poor and have things very hard, even those who find it most difficult to avoid sin: and God is going to come down and walk among the poor people of the earth, among those who are unhappy and sinful and distressed, and raise them up and make them the greatest saints and send them walking all over the universe with the steps of angels and the voices of prophets to bring His light back into the world again.

11 JUNE
Life in the world is terribly unhappy for many people. They cannot see the way out. They do not know that Christ has overcome the world.

12 JUNE
The thing is then not to struggle to work out the 'laws' of a mysterious force alien to us and utterly outside us, but to come to terms with what is inmost in our own selves, the very depth of our own being. No matter what our 'Providence' may have in store for us, on the surface of life (and this inner Providence is not really so directly concerned with the surface of life), what is within, inaccessible to the evil will of others, is always good unless we ourselves deliberately cut ourselves off from it. As for those who are too shattered to do anything about it one way or the other, they are lifted, in pieces, into heaven and find themselves together there with no sense of how it might have been possible.

13 JUNE
God is Life. God is Love. When we can get in contact with Him and when our souls wake up to the presence of the Living God and feel the touch of His fire striking at the roots of our hearts, then we begin to know what happiness really is.

14 JUNE
You ask me if I am weary? Sure. Perhaps not as weary as you are, but weary in the same way, weary of the same things. It is complicated by the fact that one is tempted to feel he has no right to be weary of the actions and pronouncements of a lot of very good, sincere people who are themselves weary of something or other. We are like a bunch of drunken men at the last end of a long stupid party falling over the furniture in the twilight of dawn. I hope it is dawn.

15 JUNE

You are at the beginning of a long and beautiful road – beautiful because it is so plain. The only thing you need to remember is not to seek your own pleasure along its way. If you seek pleasure you will never find it. If you seek to please Him, you will please yourself much more. For Jesus takes the greatest pleasure in the soul that has no greater pleasure than to please Him.

16 JUNE

But the thing that eats one up is the anguish over the Church. ... there is this conviction that the Church is full of a terrible spiritual sickness, even though there is always that inexpressible life ...

17 JUNE

This may seem strange: but sometimes, when prayer is dry, it is good and praiseworthy to look at some real created thing and *feel* and *appreciate* its reality – a flower, a tree, the woods (for you, the garden!) or even a person. (But there you had better be careful.) Just let the reality of what is real sink into you, and you find your soul spontaneously begins to pray again, for through real things we can reach Him Who is infinitely real. At the same time, we never forget that their reality is also relatively unreal and that we must not become attached to it.

18 JUNE

... What one must do is meet the needs that He brings before us, when and as He does so. We will not see anything clear, but we must do His will. We have to be heroic in our obedience to God. And that may mean cutting through a whole forest of empty talk and clichés and nonsense just to begin to find some glimmer of His will. To obey always and not know for sure if we are really obeying. That is not fun at all, and people like to get around the responsibility by entering into a routine of trivialities in which everything seems clear and noble and defined: but when you look at it honestly it falls apart, for it is riddled with absurdity from top to bottom....

19 JUNE
All is not simple and easy in the solitary life, but the thing about it is that the trials make sense and one sees that one has to go through them and put up with them, and one tries to meet it all in a constructive sort of a way. So it is work to do.

20 JUNE
Silence is the greatest luxury in the world today …

21 JUNE
I wish you all a good summer, peace, contentment, and the joy you seek: or at least the courage and light to live free from care amid unavoidable trouble! The greatness of man, Camus wrote, consists in his ability to find something bigger than himself – and he added that if we cannot expect perfect happiness in this life, we *can* measure up to this kind of greatness. Don't let the system grind you down! Joy to you in the Lord Jesus, who is our peace and our hope.

22 JUNE
We have to see not only the nothingness of things and not only their value but their nothingness and their value both at the same time. In that way we avoid a temptation of contemplatives who despise ordinary things not so much because they are nothing in the sight of God but because they are boring to ourselves. Boredom and detachment are two different things.

23 JUNE

It is at such a time as this that one has to have faith in the Church, and the fact that we suffer from the things that make us suffer, the fact that we cannot find any way out of the suffering, is perhaps a sign of hope. ... What is wanted is love. But love has been buried under words, noise, plans, projects, systems, and apostolic gimmicks. And when we open our mouths to do something about it we add more words, noise, plans, etc. We are afflicted with the disease of constant talking with almost nothing to say.

24 JUNE

But the thing that I am surest of is that I am somehow on the right track, and the path that He wants for me is the one I am walking on, and I have no need to seek another. But by the path I am walking on I mean the concrete one I am walking on, not just the institutional Cistercian path – I mean *my* path. Which oddly enough seems to be Cistercian too. And it is going into the desert but not the desert that anyone expects. It is not going anywhere that anyone expects, including myself. And that is where I want to go; and where, by God's grace, I will go.

25 JUNE

What is valuable is what is real, here and now. The present reality is the reflection of an eternal reality, and through the present we enter into eternity. That does not mean that everything becomes shadowy. The saints more than anyone else appreciate the reality and value of everyday life and of created things around them. They appreciate them not for themselves but for Jesus – in Whom they all exist.

26 JUNE
You should guarantee for yourself the peace and tranquillity in which your hearts can be open to the slightest call of grace without useless distractions. ... You should feel yourselves free from the noise and useless bustle of an over-loaded life. This means that you should preserve the spirit of solitude and avoid useless contacts with the outside.

27 JUNE
It is out of the nothing, the void, of our own self that we freely create the paradise in which we walk with God. This act of creation is – grace. It is all a gift. Grace out of nothingness.

28 JUNE
Be true to the Spirit of God and to Christ. Read your Prophets sometimes, and go through the Gospels and St. Paul and see what is said there: that is your life. You are called to a totally new, risen, transformed life in the Spirit of Christ. A life of simplicity and truth and joy that is not of this world. May you be blessed always in it ...

29 JUNE
Do not push too hard with the work, God will take care of everything, and will give you strength to do all that needs to be done. The rest is in His hands. Realize yourself to be entirely in His love and His care and worry about nothing. In these days you should be carried by Him towards your destination, and do what you do more as play than as work, which does not mean that it is not serious: for the most serious thing in the life of a Christian is play. The seriousness of Christian play is the only genuine seriousness. Our work, when it develops the seriousness of worldly accomplishment, is sad indeed, and it does nothing. But of course it is normal

to work 'against the clock' when one's time is clearly measured, and to feel anxiety about not finishing. But this too is part of God's play in our life, and we will see it in the end. It is like the book of Tobias, that beautiful book about God's play in the life of man, and in the troubles of man. All life is in reality the playing and dancing of the Child-God in His world, and we, alas, have not seen it and known it.

30 JUNE

Certainly the dimensions that faith gives to life are absolutely necessary for us to find our true selves and lose our false selves. I am glad that light and liberation have come into your life, with the Holy Spirit. Do not be surprised however if he also sometimes brings darkness and crisis. Crisis is both necessary and fruitful and the religious view of life makes crisis more fruitful, and truly so.

JULY

1 JULY

I doubt if we are called upon to accomplish anything, but we will be what *we cannot help being*. This is the great truth that at once humbles and encourages us. On the basis of this awareness, I think there is every reason for a great boldness and freedom, but in a kind of Taoist dimension of not-striving. I am struck above all by the limitless depths of despair that are really implicit in the pitiful 'hopes' of so many moderns, Christians, who are trying to come out with justifications for a completely secularised and optimistic eschatology of pseudo-science, in which the eventual triumph of religion is to discover that God is 'dead' and that there is no religion anyway. The thing that we have seen is that this discovery is so old and so childish that it has been absorbed and explained millennia ago in the apophatic tradition, which results in the most positive of all the answers and affirmations, in apparent negation …

2 JULY

We are all cracked in slightly different ways, that's all. The first thing is to accept ourselves as we are and God's grace as it is given (to learn to recognize this, one may need help, I guess), and then learn to live without too many exorbitant plans and projects for the future.

3 JULY

The problem is to distinguish between real seriousness and the pettifogging regularism that puts exaggerated emphasis on trivial externals and the letter of outdated usages, thus preventing a real return to the essence of the life, which is in solitude, silence, contemplative prayer, reflection, time to penetrate the word of God and listen to His voice, etc., etc. And of course with all this there is absolutely essential humility, compunction, self-stripping and 'self-naughting', which people seem to get away from, with their hopes of 'self-expression', though I suppose in a way this is a need too, but has to be rightly understood.

4 JULY

The great thing is to be emptied out, to taste and see that the Lord is sweet, and to learn the way of abandonment and peace. Littleness is the chief characteristic of the solitary, or else he is not a genuine solitary. Silence is a rare luxury in the modern world, and not everyone can stand it: but it has inestimable value, that cannot be purchased with any amount of money or power or intelligence. The gift to be silent and simple with the Lord is a treasure beyond counting and it almost takes care of everything else, at least in some souls.

5 JULY

To begin with I am becoming more and more convinced that true simplicity, in the depths of the heart, is almost impossible for an American or a European. Certainly they may be subjectively sincere and mean well, but the fact that they come from a society that divides man from the very start and fills him with conflicts and doubts must mean something.

6 JULY

With a great deal of prayer, humility, willingness to be changed and transformed interiorly, to be quieted down, etc. etc., and to do all the rest that God asks of you as time goes on, you will doubtless prepare to meet His grace. ... In other words, take it easy. Take what God gives and trust Him. He will do the rest.

7 JULY

For some time past the thought has been growing on me more and more that since Christianity is simple life in Christ, a life that we all share, then the more we can be conscious of that sharing and rejoice in it together, the more we will be Christians and the more we will be one in Him. And I do feel that what we all have in common is so much greater and more important than what we do not have in common, at least dogmatically and juridically. There is One Christ on earth when Christians really will to be one in mind and heart, in Him. The institutional differences are there, and they are unfortunate, but they are not stronger than charity. That is the best formula I can think of for Christian unity, and I have a strong suspicion that it has something to do with the Gospels. The rest follows from this, and must, if anything is to follow at all.

8 JULY

Personally I do not think satori is impossible for a Christian any more than it is for a Buddhist. In either case, one goes in a certain sense beyond all categories, religious or otherwise. But perhaps our very attitude toward Christianity makes this harder for us. I do think it is probably best to simply take what Zen can offer us in the way of inner purification and freedom from systems and concepts, and not worry too much about precisely where we get.

9 JULY

It seems to me that we all have an enormous amount to do just looking for what is real: and of course that has to go on all the time because you never definitively find anything that stays real in the same way the next day (except in its metaphysical ground, and that can't be 'possessed' by an individual as his 'own'). We have our life's work cut out for us just keeping real. The tragedy is to suppose that a society, an institution, a cause, or even a Church, will do the job for us. And it is rough to have to recognize that what we have been trying to build has to be taken apart and put back together in a better way – and with a lot of trouble. Yet there is always something very good about starting out all over again.

10 JULY

However, do believe me in deep union and agreement with the forces of life and hope that are struggling for the renewal of the true cultural and spiritual vitality of the 'new work' which is sometimes so tired, so old and so shabby. It is what pretends to be most 'new' that is often the oldest and weariest thing of all. But the forces of life must win. And Christians must rediscover the truth that the Cross is the sign of life, renewal, affirmation and joy, not of death, repression, negation and the refusal of life. We must not refuse the providential opportunities that come to us in the midst of darkness.

11 JULY

[On solitude] Time takes on a completely different quality and one really lives, even though nothing apparently happens at all. The direction is all vertical, and that is what matters, though at the same time one is not conscious of it.

12 JULY

Nowadays it is no longer a question of who is right, but who is at least not criminal. If any of us can say that any more. So don't worry about whether or not in every point you are perfectly right according to everybody's books: you are right before God as far as you can go and you are fighting for a truth that is clear enough and important enough. What more can anybody do?

13 JULY

I can say as a Christian, and an existentialist Christian, that I have often experienced the fact that the 'moment of truth' in the Christian context is the encounter with the inscrutable word of God, the personal and living interpretation of the word of God when it is lived, when it breaks through by surprise into our own completely contemporary and personal existence. And this means of course that it breaks through conventional religious routines and even seems in some ways quite scandalous in terms of the average and accepted interpretation of what religion ought to be.

14 JULY

I heartily recommend, as a form of prayer, the Russian and Greek business where you get off somewhere quiet, remember what you may have known about hatha-yoga, breathe quietly and rhythmically with the diaphragm, holding your breath for a bit each time and letting it out easily: and while holding it, saying 'in your heart' (aware of the place of your heart, as if the words were spoken in the very centre of your being with all the sincerity you can muster): 'Lord Jesus Christ Son of God have mercy on me a sinner'. Just keep saying this for a while, of course with faith, and the awareness of the indwelling, etc. It is a simple form of prayer, and fundamental, and the breathing part makes it easier to keep your mind on what you are doing. That's about as far as I go with methods. After that, pray as the Spirit moves you ...

15 JULY

... Do the best you can. Pray as you can, read as much as you can, find out what the monks are doing and then do what you like. The thing to avoid is getting stuck in any small limited area of Christian life: if you want to fall down on your face before God one day, that is all right, but it doesn't have to become a system to be followed thereafter until your dying day.

16 JULY

It seems to me that we create obstacles for ourselves by setting up arbitrary division, 'intellectual life' and 'life of prayer'. Each of us has to find the unity in which everything fits and takes its right place. For some, a certain amount of intellectual life is necessary for the life of prayer. Each must work out just what the right measure may be. And it varies, at different times of our life. The best thing is to acquire that discretion by which we can tell when to do what needs to be done, even though it does not seemingly fit in to some ideal plan... . There are moments when all plans are useless. So while we cannot rely on them, we learn to rely more directly on God Himself, Who cannot fail us.

17 JULY

... Obviously the ultimate destiny of each individual person is a matter of ... personal response to the truth and to the manifestation of God's will ... and not merely a matter of belonging to this or that organisation. Hence it follows that any man who follows his faith and his conscience, and responds truthfully and sincerely to what he believes to be the manifestation of the will of God, cannot help being saved by God. There is and can be no question in my mind that every sincere believer in God, no matter what may be his affiliation, if he lives according to his belief will receive mercy and, if needed, further enlightenment.

18 JULY

I return to the original idea of this letter: the joy of being able to communicate with friends, in a world where there is so much noise and very little contact. We cannot realize the extent of our trouble and our risk, and yet we do not know what to do – except to go on being human. This in itself is already an achievement. And we hope that since God became man, there is nothing greater for us than simply to be men ourselves, and persons in His image, and accept the risks and torments of a confused age. And though the age is confused, it is no sin for us to be nevertheless happy and to have hopes, provided they are not the vain and empty hopes of a world that is merely affluent …

19 JULY

I will in any case keep praying for you to the All-Merciful One, in whose hands we all are and upon whose infinite and loving wisdom we all totally depend. Let us grow in this realization of dependence and obedience to Him; this should be our great desire, to obey His truth and His love in everything and thus give Him great glory in His world where men in their madness do not know Him.

20 JULY

Yes, I think the question of solitude is very important – naturally. We need a real solitude that will empty us out, help strip us of ourselves. There is a great deal of 'vanity' (in the sense of Ecclesiastes) even in a social life that is serious and good. One needs periods of real silence, isolation, lostness, in order to be deeply convinced and aware that God is All. Without experience of that, our prayer life is so thin.

21 JULY

… One thing strikes me and moves me most of all. It is the idea of the *'point vierge, ou le desespoir accule le coeur de l'excommunie'* ['the virginal point, the centre of the soul, where despair corners the heart of the outsider']. What a very fine analysis, and how true. We in our turn have to reach that same *'point vierge'* in a kind of despair at the hypocrisy of our own world. It is dawning more and more on me that I have been caught in civilization as in a kind of spider's web, and I am beginning to say 'No' louder and louder, though surrounded by the solicitude of those who ask me why I do so. There is no way of explaining it, and perhaps not even time to do so.

22 JULY

However, no one is exempt from anguish. I share the agony of spirits you speak of, and for the same reasons.

23 JULY

There is no doubt that we are all involved in a social structure that is rotting from within. The fact that so many good people are able to identify this futile and transient structure with Christian civilisation or even, worse still, the body of Christ, is enough to cause anyone agony. I think this agony is simply the inevitable form our suffering takes at such a time. We feel useless, bound, helpless … We are stopped, blocked, tongue-tied. When we open our mouths we run into so much contra-diction that we wonder whether or not we can believe our own convictions. As Christians we are not really 'with' any of the big social movements in one direction or another, left or right. We no longer have the support of a really Christian society. When we lean on the society that is built on what used to be Christian, it gives way and we fall with it ... yet we cannot commit ourselves to the even more transient secularism that claims to possess the key to the future.

24 JULY

On another level, the level of religion and faith, which nevertheless enters into universal being as we know and experience it, is God Who does not really form part of 'being' and is in a sense entirely other than any being we are capable of knowing, so that we can only pass from being to Him by a kind of inexplicable breakthrough. The Zens do it in Satori, we do it by Christian faith, and in neither case is there any point in my trying to justify it to you. You either do or you don't.

25 JULY

I think we can accept ourselves as we are, and differences in terminology and exoteric formulation are of course neither underestimated nor overestimated. All this is perfectly taken for granted, and poses not the slightest problem ...

26 JULY

The Church is not of this world, and she complacently reminds us of this when we try to budge her in any direction. But on the other hand we also are of the Church and we also have our duty to speak up and say the Church is not of this world when her refusal to budge turns out, in effect, to be a refusal to budge from a solidly and immovably temporal position.

27 JULY

The way toward the Homeland becomes more and more obscure. As I look back over the stages which were once more clear, I see that we are all on the right road, and though it be night, it is a saving one. We are very much alone, as regards the crowd which presses in around us. But as regards that 'cloud of witnesses', well, that is something altogether different …

28 JULY

I can depend less and less on my own power and sense of direction – as if I ever had any. But the Lord supports and guides me without my knowing how, more and more apart from my own action and even in contradiction to it. It is so strange to advance backwards and to get where you are going in a totally unexpected way.

29 JULY

To be a contemplative is to be in some ways maladjusted and even though by forcing oneself, one can put up with the superficialities and pretences of social life, one constantly sees through them and is very aware of their absurdity and meaninglessness. To live in a state of more or less unrelieved absurdity is certainly not pleasant, and one suffers loneliness, frustration, confusion, and besides, one is always getting into somewhat humiliating situations because of it. However, that does not mean that we cannot function fairly smoothly and get along with people. Yet I for one (although I am thought to be very friendly and spontaneous) am always fairly well aware of the falsity of most 'conventional' social relationships and the double talk that one has to indulge in, pretending that it all makes sense when it is really ludicrous.

30 JULY

I think some active charitable work is good for the contemplative life, provided that we don't get into it purely out of restlessness and aimlessness. In everything, however, the great thing is God's will. A contemplative is one who has God's will bearing right down upon him, often in the most incomprehensible way. One feels that if one could only *see* clearly *how* it was God's will, the whole thing would be less painful. But it just is, and there is no explanation. This is painful. God is to us painful Himself, and we are to ourselves painful, during a great deal of our life. But we must not make too much of it, and I prefer not to think about it or talk about it.

31 JULY

I am sick up to the teeth and beyond the teeth, up to the eyes and beyond the eyes, with all forms of projects and expectations and statements and programmes and explanations of anything, especially explanations about where we are all going, because where we are all going is where we went a long time ago, over the falls. We are in a new river and we don't know it.

AUGUST

1 AUGUST

So we continue to live and try to seek truth. Each must do so with courage and indefatigable patience, constantly discerning it from the obsessive fictions of the establishment everywhere ...

2 AUGUST

You should not be in confusion or in doubt, but open your hearts to the Holy Spirit and rejoice in His freedom which no man can take from you. No power on earth can keep you from loving God and from union with Him. Nor need you depend on the devotionalism of the past. The Lord is near to you and lives in you. His Gospel is not old and forgotten, it is new, and it is there for you to meditate. By His grace you can still come to the sacraments of the Church, and rejoice that you are in the Body of Christ.

3 AUGUST

Progress in Prayer ... is a ticklish subject because the chief obstacle to progress is too much self-awareness and to talk about 'how to make progress' is a good way to make people too aware of themselves. In the long run I think progress in prayer comes from the Cross and humiliation and whatever makes us really experience our total poverty and nothingness, and also gets our mind off ourselves.

4 AUGUST

What is vitally important is that you should be a Christian and as faithful to the truth as you can get. This may mean anything but resembling some of the pious faithful. But I don't have to tell you, because you know, that there is only one thing that is of any importance in your life. Call it fidelity to conscience, or to the inner voice, or to the Holy Spirit: but it involves a lot of struggle and no supineness and you probably won't get much encouragement from anybody … you have to find it as best you can. I can't necessarily tell you where to look, or how much of it you have found already. The start of it all is that none of us really have started to look. But the mercy of God, unknown and caricatured and blasphemed by some of the most reputable squares, is the central reality out of which all the rest comes and into which all the rest returns.

5 AUGUST

… I realize that I am about at the end of some kind of a line. What line? What is the trolley I am probably getting off? The trolley is called a special kind of hope. The streetcar of expectation, of proximately to be fulfilled desire of betterment, of things becoming much more intelligible, of things being set in a new kind of order, and so on. Point one, things are not going to get better. Point two, things are going to get worse. I will not dwell on point two. Point three, I don't need to be on the trolley car anyway, I don't belong riding in a trolley. You can call the trolley anything you like, I have got off it.

6 AUGUST

… Yes, all the monastic traditions have this in common: total liberation and availability to 'let go' and open up to the unspoken silence in which all is said: *qui erat et qui est et qui venturus est* [who was and who is and who shall come].

7 AUGUST

… The main idea is of crucial significance: namely, liberation of/from consciousness … Of all religions, Christianity is the one that least needs techniques, or least needs to depend on them. Nor is the overemphasis on sacraments necessary either: the great thing is faith. With a pure faith, our use of techniques, our understanding of the psyche and our use of the sacraments all become really meaningful. Without it, they are just routines.

8 AUGUST

There are moments when I seem to be very near despair, as I see my faults and take note of how far all of us are from this ideal here where one seems to be plunging more and more into materialism. But I see that the question is not to understand but to obey and love. God sees everything, and He can bring everything to a good end. He wants it!

9 AUGUST

We should in a way fear for our perseverance because there is a big hole in us, an abyss, and we have to fall through it into emptiness, but the Lord will catch us. Who can fall through the centre of himself into that nothingness and not be appalled? But the Lord will catch us. He will catch you without fail and take you to His Heart.

10 AUGUST

In the end, no theory that neglects real people can be of any value. It is in those that He sends to you that you see Him and love Him, and there you have a reality which cannot be taken away, a treasure like the one for which St. Lawrence died on the gridiron. You have Christ …

11 AUGUST

We (society at large) have lost our sense of values and our vision. We despise everything that Christ loves, everything marked with His compassion. We love fatness health bursting smiles the radiance of satisfied bodies all properly fed and rested and sated and washed and perfumed and sexually relieved. Anything else is a horror and a scandal to us. How sad.

12 AUGUST

Inexorably the sad things of life bear down upon us. But Christ Himself has suffered them and suffers them in us. As we drift away from the contentment of healthy and thoughtless people, and enter into the sea of perils, Christ takes hold of us. His comfort and His presence are more than health and joy. They are a greater reality. The world does not see this, and we are hardly able to believe it when we are the ones concerned. But this darkness too is a poverty which He loves in us.

13 AUGUST

How beautiful and simple God's plan for humankind is! That's it. Friends, who love, who suffer, who search, who see God's joy, who live in the glory of God; and all around them, the world which does not understand that it too is Proverb, which does not find the Lord's joy, which seems to seek to self-destruct, which despairs of rising above material things. That wants to destroy itself in the fire, despairing that it can soar above material things.

14 AUGUST

… The hermit life is no joke at all, and no picnic, but in it one gradually comes face to face with the awful need of self-emptying and even of a kind of annihilation so that God may be all, and also the apparent impossibility of it. And of course the total folly of trying to find ways of doing it oneself. The great comfort is in the goodness and sweetness and nearness of all God has made, and the created isness which makes Him first of all present in us, speaking us. Then that other word: 'Follow…'

15 AUGUST

God seeks Himself in us, and the aridity and sorrow of our heart is the sorrow of God who is not known in us, who cannot find Himself in us because we do not dare to believe or trust the incredible truth that He could live in us, and live there out of choice, out of preference. But indeed we exist solely for this, to be the place He has chosen for His presence, His manifestation in the world, His epiphany.

16 AUGUST

Nothing is more important than prayer and union with God, no matter where we may be. Christ is the source and the only source of charity and spiritual life. We can do nothing without Him and His Spirit, and I know you are now, as always, seeking no other Mover than the Spirit of Christ. That is why the Cross will cast its shadow, still, over your life. But then, in that shadow, you will see the Light of Christ, the Light of the Resurrection. He lives in us, and through our poverty He must reign. And I need not tell you how poor He makes us in order to reign in us. If we knew how poor and desolate we would have to be when we began to follow Him, perhaps we would have fallen back.

17 AUGUST

The Truth that makes us free is not merely a matter of information about God but the presence in us of a divine person by love and grace, bringing us into the intimate personal life of God as His Sons by adoption. This is the basis of all prayer and all prayer should be oriented to this mystery… in which the Spirit in us recognises the Father. The cry of the Spirit in us, the cry of recognition that we are Sons in the Son, is the heart of our prayer and the great motive of prayer.

18 AUGUST
Now, as always, God's real work remains obscure and humble in the eyes of the world. Now more than ever, we have to be suspicious of results that are achieved by the efficient, over-efficient technological means of which the world is so proud. Christ works always humbly and almost in the dark, but never more than now …

19 AUGUST
The contemplative has nothing to tell you except to reassure you and say that if you dare to penetrate your own silence and risk the sharing of that solitude with the lonely other who seeks God through you, then you will truly recover the light and the capacity to understand what is beyond words and beyond explanations because it is too close to be explained: it is the intimate union in the depths of your own heart, of God's spirit and your own secret inmost self, so that you and He are in all truth One Spirit. I love you, in Christ.

20 AUGUST
We have got to be people of hope, and to be so we have to see clearly how true it is that the hopes of a materialistic culture are the worst form of despair. We have to build a new world, and yet resist the world while representing Christ in the midst of it.

21 AUGUST

In the language familiar to me as a Catholic monk, it is as if we were known to one another in God. This is a very simple and to me obvious expression for something quite normal and ordinary, and I feel no need to apologise for it. I am convinced that you understand me perfectly. It is true that a person always remains a person and utterly separate and apart from every other person. But it is equally true that each person is destined to reach with others an understanding and a unity which transcend individuality, and Russian tradition describes this with a concept we do not fully possess in the West – *sobornost.*

22 AUGUST

… I have learned to rejoice that Jesus is in the world in people who know Him not, that He is at work in them when they think themselves far from Him, and it is my joy to tell you to hope though you think that for you of all men hope is impossible. Hope not because you think you can be good, but because God loves us irrespective of our merits and whatever is good in us comes from His love, not from our own doing.

23 AUGUST

Thus we are left as children, as the saved remnant which is forgotten, we are like the animals in Noah's ark, which floats off on the waves of the deluge of materialism without anyone but God knowing where we will end up.

24 AUGUST

Our lives go on, at times it seems they are fruitless. We must always pray to be attuned to the mysterious language of events, and shape our actions accordingly. It requires prayer and humility and vigilance and love. Although it says in

Ecclesiastes that there is nothing new under the sun, yet there is always the creative newness of our decisions, in the service of God. May they be filled with His Spirit and with His 'new life'.

In any case, let us pray for one another that we may make creative use of the mysterious difficulties of life and shape our courses in 'new directions' if that be the will of God. I fear nothing so much as conventionalism and inertia, which for me is fatal. Yet there is that all-important stillness, and listening to God, which seems to be inertia, and yet is the highest action. One must always be awake to tell the difference between action and inaction, when appearances are so often deceiving …

25 AUGUST

Look, if you think about darkness you will naturally get a tired mind. And if you think about it you put a kind of light in its place, that is what makes you tired. When it is dark, it is dark, and you go in the dark as if it were light. *Nox illuminatio mea*. The darkness is our light, and that is all. The light remains, simply, our everyday mind, such as it is, floating on a sea of darkness which we do not have to observe. But it carries us with great power. It is the being carried that is, actually, its light. Float, then. And trust the winds of God, which you do not see either, but they are cool.

26 AUGUST

You have entered into the great mystery of the Cross which no one comprehends and which one should speak of only in few words, and in a low tone, as it were in passing, with reverence and with fear.

All I can do then is to stand mutely by your side, and nod to you, and try to be encouraging. And my heart prays for you.

The Holy One Who dwells in us prays in me for you. May He answer His own prayer to give you strength and to enrich your trial with His special grace.

27 AUGUST

When you feel particularly low, and are convinced that you have been abandoned by God because of your weaknesses, remember that He is nearer then than in many an hour of consolation. Console yourself with the thought that it cannot help being that way, because God tries those whom He loves and He is close to them that are in tribulation. Both these thoughts are revealed in Scripture …

28 AUGUST

… Perhaps in my solitude I have become as it were an explorer for you, a searcher in realms which you are not able to visit…. I have been summoned to explore a desert area of man's heart in which explanations no longer suffice, and in which one learns that only experience counts. An arid, rocky, dark land of the soul, sometimes illuminated by strange fires which men fear and peopled by spectres which men studiously avoid except in their nightmares. And in this area I have learned that one cannot truly know hope unless he has found out how like despair hope is.

29 AUGUST

About prayer: have you a garden or somewhere that you can walk in, by yourself? Take half an hour, or fifteen minutes a day and just walk up and down among the flowerbeds with the intention of offering this walk up as a meditation and a prayer to Our Lord. Do not try to think about anything in particular and when thoughts about work, etc. come to you, do not try to push them out by main force, but see if you can't drop them just by relaxing your mind. Do this because you 'are praying' and because Our Lord is with you. But if thoughts about work will not go away, accept them idly and without too much eagerness with the intention of letting Our Lord reveal His will to you through these thoughts. But do not grab at anything that looks like a light. If it is a 'light' it will have its effect without your seizing it forcefully ...

30 AUGUST

... I have very rapidly discovered that what I am seeking is not eremitism or spirituality or contemplation but simply God. Also that He lets Himself be sought in order to be found, and that all the realities that have been proposed about the desert are real indeed, and not illusion, except that in my case if I think too much about 'desert' and 'eremitism' it does become a bit of a delusion. It is much simpler just to be an ordinary Christian who is living alone, as it happens. But certainly this ability to expand and move in emptiness, out of the rather confining and limited structure of the community, is an enormous blessing. I am grateful to God every moment for it, and will not spoil it by imagining that my life is in any way special, for that does indeed poison everything.

31 AUGUST

We have got to travel in the void and be perfectly happy about it. This is what actually brings to the fore the idea of *epectasis*, but it underlies everything. All that we know clearly is insufficient. We must pass on to the unknown. The hunger for God cannot be satisfied except in the sense that an entirely new dimension makes the void itself our satiation, and this is nonsense as expressed here. *Who is there left to satisfy?*

Why not cry out to God in any way you like, as long as you don't expect it to console you.

SEPTEMBER

1 SEPTEMBER

I know that God loves me much, and that He has been very patient with me. My life becomes more and more a question of graces and a confession of my wretchedness. I know that I am not a saint, but I am happy because God loves me and draws me towards Him always – He who is the Father of the poor …

2 SEPTEMBER

But the language of Christianity has been so used and so misused that sometimes you distrust it: you do not know whether or not behind the word 'Cross' there stands the experience of mercy and salvation, or only the threat of punishment. If my word means anything to you, I can say to you that I have experienced the Cross to mean mercy and not cruelty, truth and not deception: that the news of the truth and love of Jesus is indeed the true good news, but in our time it speaks out in strange places.

3 SEPTEMBER

In any event, in this world where money and power threaten to destroy everything, it is necessary to unite oneself with the innocent and the poor sinners which we all are, it is necessary to know how to be nothing more because the Saviour lives and suffers in those who are left to depend on their self to live in others and in God.

4 SEPTEMBER

Love is the epiphany of God in our poverty. The contemplative life is then the search for peace not in an abstract exclusion of all outside reality, not in a barren negative closing of the senses upon the world, but in the openness of love. It begins with the acceptance of my own self in my poverty and my nearness to despair in order to recognise that where God is there can be no despair, and God is in me even if I despair.

5 SEPTEMBER

I think of you often and keep you in my prayers. The grinding ruggedness of our lives in varying degrees of loneliness may sometimes seem grim but really I don't think we would ever settle for an exchange with the comfortable vacuity that seems to be the alternative. We should be proud of our vocation to the unusual, the lonely and the absurd (for it really has meaning).

6 SEPTEMBER

Christ in the world today is not white, nor black either: but He is certainly present and suffering in the black people and coloured people of the earth. The white world is purely and simply under judgement. And they don't know it.

7 SEPTEMBER

… I am completely convinced that for some people the only thing is a solitary and 'unattached' life. To simply go where the wind blows them, which is into various new deserts. With absolutely NO plans for any kind of structure, community, what to do, how to do it, but to simply seek the most desolate rock or the most abandoned island and sit there until the tourists move in, then to move on.

8 SEPTEMBER

I know what you are trying to say about loving God more than anything that exists but at the same time this is a measure of self-preservation. Beyond all is a love of God in and through all that exists. We must not hold them apart one from the other. But He must be One in all and Is. There comes a time when one loses everything, even love. Apparently. Even oneself, above all oneself. And this will take care of the rapture and all the rest because who will there be to be rapt?

9 SEPTEMBER

It is true that the yen for absolute solitude is often vitiated by pure narcissism, regression, immaturity, and is utterly sick. This does not alter the fact that there are vocations to solitude, and for these there remains only the question: when do I start? And how? Once artificial barriers are removed the question tends to answer itself.

10 SEPTEMBER

We sometimes forget the real dimensions of our life. There must be long 'dead' periods; they are necessary. But they may suddenly blossom out into unusual life, if we let them!

11 SEPTEMBER

... My own feeling is that Christian thought is largely hampered by fear, and does not dare to do what we, in the Holy Spirit, ought to be most ready to do: to realize our *immediate* union with God in the order of grace. ... We have not known and tasted the things that have been given to us in Christ. Instead we have built around ourselves walls and offices and cells and chambers of all sorts, and filled them full of bureaucratic litter, and buried ourselves in dust and documents, and now we wonder why we cannot see God, or leap to do His will ...

12 SEPTEMBER

The answer – the only answer I know – is that of Staretz Zossima in *The Brothers Karamazov* – to be responsible to everybody, to take upon oneself *all* the guilt – but I don't know what that means. It is romantic, and I believe it is true. But what is it? Behind it all is the secret that love has an infinite power, and its power, once released, can in an instant destroy and swallow up all hatred, all evil, all injustice, all that is diabolical. That is the meaning of Calvary.

13 SEPTEMBER

In the end, it comes to the old story that we are sinners, but that this is our hope because sinners are the ones who attract to themselves the infinite compassion of God. To be a sinner, to want to be pure, to remain in patient expectation of the divine mercy and above all to forgive and love others, as best we can, this is what makes us Christians. The great tragedy is that we feel so keenly that love has been twisted out of shape in us and beaten down and crippled. But Christ loves in us, and the compassion of Our Lady keeps her prayer burning like a lamp in the depths of our being. That lamp does not waver. It is the light of the Holy Spirit, invisible, and kept alight by her love for us.

14 SEPTEMBER

For me the wind blows to Asia …

The Asians have this only: that for thousands of years they have worked on a very complex and complete mental discipline, which is not so much aimed at separating matter from spirit, as identifying the true self and separating it from an illusion generated by society and by imaginary appetite.

15 SEPTEMBER

Grace (we say glibly) works on nature, and can work suddenly if it pleases. But actually a deep interior revolution needs to go on and this takes time. A settling and a sort of ageing of the strong new wine. We have no adequate idea of what takes place in our depths when we grow spiritually or change. ... Let peace have time to settle and gain a firm grasp of those depths. And do not be troubled if you do not always feel settled. Time takes care of such things. And the Church with her sacraments, while doing infinitely much in your life, will not take away all anguish. On the contrary, the anguish must always be there. But it must deepen and change and become vastly more fruitful. That is the best we can hope for nowadays: a fruitful anguish instead of one that is utterly sterile and consuming.

16 SEPTEMBER

Perhaps God wants you to experience contemplation in a deeply African way, which I would surmise to be a way of wholeness, a way of unity with all life, a sense of the deep rhythm of natural and cosmic life as the manifestation of God's creative power: and also a great warmth of love and praise. If you realize that God has indeed given you His Spirit as the source of all joy and strength, and trust Him to purify your heart with His presence and love, in great simplicity, He will teach you the joy of being a child of God, an African child of God with your own special unique gifts.

17 SEPTEMBER

I am realizing more and more that my big task is within myself. This is imperative. I am seeing what are the depths of my pride, and what an awful obstacle it is. In the old days I used to think about this problem in unrealistic terms:

confusing pride with vanity. I know I still have vanity enough, but now for the first time I am beginning to see into the naked depths of pride. There is something one cannot explain in words: this tenacious attachment to self, and the virulence of it, which would make one stop at *nothing* in order to protect this inner root of self. And to see that I do in fact do all sorts of evil, properly camouflaged, in defence of this root of self. The problem is that it is all tied up with our clinging to life itself, which of course is a good thing. The desire to *be*. But the desire in us is not only to be, but to be our own idol, to be our own end.

18 SEPTEMBER

Really I think that we who have sought our identity in the monastery and found it in the Cross of Christ (there is no otherwhere) must be strong to defend our freedom against every wind of doctrine and the fashions of people who run in all directions and want us to run with them: we have our own way to go, a way of freedom and hiddenness and non-production, and we need to appreciate the peculiar joys and hazards of life in the desert, the paradise-wilderness, the loneliness and love which is our own special way. It is good to hear from the other pilgrims behind the hills of sand over there …

19 SEPTEMBER

I am now pushing fifty and realize more and more that every extra day is just a free gift, and so I relax and forget about past and future. The 'I' that goes from day to day is not an important 'I' and his future matters little. And the deeper 'I' is in an eternal present. If a door should one day open from one realm to the other, then 'I' (whoever that is) will be glad of it. I have no regrets except for sins that are forgiven in any case, and I forget the past, and don't get too excited about either the present or the future. For the rest, He Who is real will take care of what reality He has shared with us.

20 SEPTEMBER

As I go on, and as friends die … I think more seriously of the deep value of a repentant life. … The thing is just so deep and so serious. Well, one just laughs a lot less. And the running around, the superficiality of so many well-meant efforts at making things new seems quite pitiful at times. So beside the point. … Fortunately, one also sees the greatness of God and His immense mercy. Then there comes a way of just being quiet, just 'shutting up' and minding one's own business which is to listen.

21 SEPTEMBER

But it certainly is a wonderful thing to wake up suddenly in the solitude of the woods and look up at the sky and see the utter nonsense of *everything*, including all the solemn stuff given out by professional asses about the spiritual life: and simply to burst out laughing, and laugh and laugh, with the sky and the trees because God is not in words, and not in systems, and not in liturgical movements, and not in 'contemplation' with a big C, or in asceticism or in anything like that, not even in the apostolate. Certainly not in books. I can go on writing them, for all that, but one might as well make paper airplanes out of the whole lot.

22 SEPTEMBER

Above all, trust (hope). The virtue of hope is the one talented people most need. They tend to trust in themselves – and when their own resources fail then they will prefer despair to reliance on anyone else, even on God. It gives them a kind of feeling of distinction.

23 SEPTEMBER

In the end, though, the solution is Love – you have said it. And love, it seems to me, implies the realization that perhaps already those subject to us know our failings very well, and accept them with love, and would not dream of holding them against us, because they know these things do not matter. That is the great consolation: in the joy of being known and forgiven, we find it so much easier to forgive everything, even before it happens.

24 SEPTEMBER

There is only one solution: that Christ Himself, in us, must be the Superior, for He alone is worthy. And we must be content to struggle to keep out of His way. Above all, as you say so wisely, we must be glad if those under us *see* our defects, and are even aware of our sins in some way. Because that means that they will not expect too much from us, and will place their hopes in Christ. The crux of the whole 'problem' of being a Superior is right there, in the shame we feel at letting everyone down, the shame at not being up to our task, the fear that everything will be known, that our nothingness will be seen and realized.

25 SEPTEMBER

You can pull my leg all you want, it stretches indefinitely, and we both understand quite well the way in which you belong to Christ. We both belong to Him in His mercy which is inscrutable and infinite and reaches into the inmost depths of every being, but especially of all who, with all their deficiencies and limitations, seek only truth and love, as best they can.

26 SEPTEMBER

I find I simply do not have the power to go on doing many things. I have to stop and vegetate. Eventually I may take root and turn into a plant.

27 SEPTEMBER

Certainly you are right about 'doing nothing' and all things coming out of it. And that we ought not to be preoccupied with doing 'things'. This thing and that. I am certainly going more and more in that direction.

28 SEPTEMBER

The hermit life is a kind of walking on water, in which one no longer can account for anything but one knows that one has not drowned and that this is to nobody's credit but God's …

One does have to cut loose and float away without ties, in one way or other …

29 SEPTEMBER

I do not understand too much of any kind of Church which is made up entirely of people whose external conformity has made them comfortable and secure, and has given them the privilege of looking down on everybody else who is automatically 'wrong' because not conformed to them. This does not seem to me to have a great deal to do with the message of Christ.

30 SEPTEMBER

… The world is lying inert under a huge weight of spiritual torpor and heaviness, with conscience gone dead and all awareness extinct. And the disaster hangs over all … . This is indeed the time for purity of heart, compunction and detachment, to embrace the truth. I still do not see clearly what to look for!

OCTOBER

1 OCTOBER

As for the call to solitude it is in some respects unavoidable, and imperative, and even if you are prevented by circumstances (e.g., marriage!) from doing anything about it, solitude will come and find you anyway, and this is not always the easiest thing in life either. It may take the form of estrangement, and really it shouldn't. But it does. However, that should not be sought or even too eagerly consented to. On the contrary. In any case the right result should be a great purity of heart and selflessness and detachment.

2 OCTOBER

… I wish I could explain to you what gets into my heart and simply carries me away. The Mass has done it more than anything else. But all of a sudden I have seen what it *means* to be a member of Christ, and have developed a sense of what we are all made for and heading for, that wonderful union in Him, 'that they may be one as Thou Father and I are one, that they may be one in us … Thou in me and I in them'. I have begun to long for the perfection of that union with an anguish that is sometimes almost physical.

3 OCTOBER

All of us who are called to a serious way of life are called to face the blackness of ourselves and of our world. If we have to live the victory of the Risen Christ over death we have to pass through death. Or arise out of our own death. It means seeing death and hell in ourselves. I never imagined when I was a novice and when 'His lamp shone over my head' what it would mean to suffer the darkness which He Himself suffers in me. Filthy? We are utterly abominable and vile, all of us. How we can get through a day without constant retching is to me almost incomprehensible. But on the other hand it is not His will that we make much of this either. Simply accept it as our ordinary state. I wonder if you have ever run across the remarkable Athos mystic of our century, Staretz Silouan. He died in 1938, a Russian, at the Rossiko on Mt. Athos. The Lord told him once: 'Keep your soul in hell and do not despair'. This is a bit far from the hearts-and-flowers mysticism of our western victim souls, but it is very true, for if we descend into hell in this life we do not have to worry about it in the next. Nor is it really a matter of much choice. We *are* in hell. But a hell we can get out of if we don't try to transform it into heaven or pretend that it is heaven.

4 OCTOBER

We know that our heavenly Father has a very special concern for the poor and the abandoned, who are the apple of His eye. We know that He pays very special attention to the needs of those whom the world ought to care for, but whom the world tends to reject.

5 OCTOBER

We have a vocation *not* to be disturbed by the turmoil and wreckage of the great fabric of illusions. Naturally we must suffer and feel to some extent lost in the tempest, for we cannot be complacently 'out' of it. And yet we are, because of Him who dwells in us. But precisely in Him and by Him we are deeply involved by compassion: yet compassion is useless without freedom. I am sure our desire to understand this paradox and live in fidelity to it is the best indication that we can have the grace to do so. But none of it will come from our (outward) selves …

6 OCTOBER

If I can presume that the Lord wishes to speak through me in any way, I would say He wants us all to know not to punish ourselves and not to be Satan to ourselves. Let us accuse no one, punish no one, accuse ourselves rightly of course, but not as Satan does: rather as the woman with the issue of blood, who 'accused' herself by touching the hem of His garment in secret and with many, many tears, almost despairing yet hoping tremendously. This alone is our joy. Let us not swallow it back and be afraid of it. Let it burst out of us, and not remain imprisoned within us, for if it be imprisoned in our hearts our very joy will punish us …

7 OCTOBER

… I think that any attempt whatever to sincerely discover a genuine centre of meaning for one's life, a centre that in some way or other is seen as 'superior' to one's empirical, everyday, inauthentic existence, must have something to do with grace. Any attempt that sincerely seeks the ground of our being and the ultimate purpose of existence in a 'disinterested' manner (i.e., not as a form of self-affirmation that simply reinforces one's superficial egoism) seems to me to very probably have some relation to grace.

8 OCTOBER

There is great joy if we do not play the devil's role and punish ourselves and one another. The great secret is to be other than devils. That is why we must be meek and loving even toward ourselves, especially toward ourselves. The fourth degree of love is to love ourselves as, and because, God loves us. This too I have learned or begun to learn in hell. Oh, the mercy of God. We are its ministers, even for ourselves. We must minister mercy to our hateful self, and to our brother in whom we most see our own condition reflected. Thus we become Christs, in no other way can we.

9 OCTOBER

Really I do not feel myself in opposition with anyone or with any form of spirituality, because I no longer think in such terms at all: this spirituality is *the* right kind, that is *the* wrong kind, etc. Right sort and wrong sort: these are sources of delusion in the spiritual life and there precisely is where the Buddhists score, for they bypass all that. Neither this side of the stream nor on the other side: yet one must cross the stream and throw away the boat, before seeing that the stream wasn't there.

10 OCTOBER

But believe me when the angels and saints appear among us they don't appear in rich men's houses, and the place I want to be is somewhere where the angels are not only present but even sometimes visible: that is slums, or Trappist monasteries, or where there are children, or where there is one guy starving himself in a desert for sorrow and shame at the sins and injustices of the world.

11 OCTOBER

In my opinion the job of the Christian is to try to give an example of sanity, independence, human integrity, good sense, as well as Christian love and wisdom, against all establishments and all mass movements and all current fashions which are merely mindless and hysterical. But of course are they? And do we get hung up in merely futile moral posturing? Well, somewhere we have to choose. The most popular and exciting thing at the moment is not necessarily the best choice.

12 OCTOBER
Those of us who have chosen to seek God in the desert of the contemplative life have ample experience of the emptiness of so many slogans, proofs, declarations, and so on that are made about Him. On the other hand I must say that we also have learned in some measure to experience the great paradox that when He is 'absent' He is in a way most 'present'.

13 OCTOBER
The world is going through a terrible spiritual crisis and we all have to suffer for the stupidity of the past centuries and for our own. Sometimes I think that only the psalms and the prophets and Job can articulate our anguish in an adequate way. Christ Himself who suffered in them, is suffering in us. All humanity inexorably climbs to Calvary with the Lord, either as the repentant thief, or as the other or, what is worse, as the Pharisees. As for us, I hope we are repentant thieves, we must be very united with each other in our humility and poverty and strength – united, too, with all of history's poor, the poets of the psalms like the Indian poets. We are all Christ, and we have to know it and be witnesses of the truth and the mystery.

14 OCTOBER
Calcutta is a shattering experience. I wish everybody could see it. Incredible – and *not* beautiful really, certainly not 'fun'. The poverty is staggering. The filth, misery, disease, crowding, despair, overwhelms you. … Makes you realize that

you can't judge the world by America and Europe. We are Dives and they are Lazarus! The experience of being in the midst of such human misfortune really makes you think about the importance of deep prayer. For things like this, 'action' in our sense of the word is helpless. Revolution would only bring madness and cruelty, but no solution. The sense that all this is there and you can do *nothing* that makes sense. … It has really got me shook up! The only answer is prayer and fasting. When you see so many hungry people you feel funny about eating so well!

15 OCTOBER

This is what … will now require the most prayers and the greatest help of the Holy Spirit. A work of God can often and usually does demand a complete uprooting that is extremely painful and disconcerting, and which requires great fidelity in the one called to do the work. The difficulty comes in the darkness and possibility of doubt, in the mystical risk involved. … But we will all have to be very determined and struggle without discouragement, trusting in God and accepting difficulty and delay.

16 OCTOBER

We know what being, power, etc., are in the world of experience, but the things that we thus know are so infinitely far from the 'being', etc., of God that it is just as true to say that God is 'no-being' as to say that He is 'being'.

17 OCTOBER

We live in difficult times, but we are in the hands of a merciful and wise Father. He guides our destinies, He brings salutary medicine for our sins. The world faces much suffering. May we all be faithful to His grace …

18 OCTOBER

… I think we make problems for ourselves where there really are none. There is too much conscious 'spiritual life' floating around us, and we are too aware that we are supposed to get somewhere. Well, where? If you reflect, the answer turns out to be a word that is never very close to any kind of manageable reality. If that is the case, perhaps we are already in that where. In which case why do we torment ourselves looking around to verify a fact which we cannot see in any case? We should let go our hold upon our self and our will, and be in the Will in which we are. Contentment is very important, of course I mean what seems to be contentment with despair. And the worst thing of all is false optimism.

19 OCTOBER

Let us be united in our prayers. This I say not as a formula, but in desperate poverty and need. With everyone else who is in need, who is an exile, a captive, who hungers for truth and cannot find truth, let us pray and mourn in our hearts and cry out to God, the God of Abraham, the God also of Agar and Ishmael. May He give you strength in your sufferings and may His angels stand guard over you at all times. May the Holy Mother of God console you. May the Saviour of the world bless you.

20 OCTOBER

Really I am sure that if we are patient something good will come up. You must realize that it is the ordinary way of God's dealings with us that our ideas do not work out speedily and efficiently as we would like them to. The reason for this is not only the loving wisdom of God, but also the fact that our acts have to fit into a great complex pattern that we cannot possibly understand. I have learned over the years that Providence is always a whole lot wiser than any of us, and that there are always not only good reasons but the very *best* reasons for the delays and blocks that often seem to us so frustrating and absurd.

21 OCTOBER

It seems to me that the law of love is written by nature itself in the heart of man. The command to love God and our fellow man does not come to us out of the blue somewhere. It is implied in our very being. For me, the experience of love is rooted first of all in a deep sense of the value of *being*. I think that if we once realize what it means that we *are*, and that we have received the gift of life, whereas we need not have come into being at all, and if we see that this is a pure gift of God who is Himself pure Being, then we begin to see that in making us 'be' He has given us a participation in His own being, and called us also to be His own children. But it is by the additional gift of grace that He makes us aware of ourselves as His sons in Christ. It seems to me that if we learn to experience the meaning of these gifts in our own lives, there is no further problem about loving God and other men who share the same gifts and the same finalities. The reasons are not to be sought outside ourselves: if we learn to listen to our own hearts, and keep those hearts true in the faith of the Church, we will hear the answers.

22 OCTOBER

As for your prayer: we have to face the fact that man is naturally a little lazy and doesn't *like* to pray a lot of the time. We bring useless trouble upon ourselves if we imagine that we must always be sweetly and passively attracted to prayer, and that if we are not something is wrong. No: we are more often than not cold and dull. But we have to revive our prayer with real acts of *faith*. Faith is the virtue which really puts us in contact with God: the true God, the living God ... He is always there, even when He is not felt. Finally, we owe Him our sincere efforts and He does not owe us any results or any satisfaction in return, and so we should be perfectly happy to make a lot of efforts without any apparent result …

23 OCTOBER

Well, my friend, we live in troubled and sad times, and we must pray the infinite and merciful Lord to bear patiently with the sins of this world, which are very great. We must humble our hearts in silence and poverty of spirit and listen to His commands which come from the depths of His love, and work that … hearts may be converted to the ways of love and justice, not of blood, murder, lust and greed. I am afraid that the big powerful countries are a very bad example to the rest of the world in this respect.

24 OCTOBER

Believing is not only *not seeing* but it is also a staunch refusal to say you see what you don't see. I was a non-believer until the day it dawned on me that the absolute void of nothingness in which I could not possibly see anything or hear anything was also the absolute fullness of everything. This was not so much a religious insight as a metaphysical or Zen-like one, and the religious implications followed later, without changing the essentially negative view (since there cannot possibly be an adequate idea of God). To put it crudely, your 'unnamed something' without ceasing to be pure Nothing suddenly ran over me like a truck.

25 OCTOBER

So, friend … I am not Father Merton inside the warm Church calling you to come and sit by the fire of positive thinking or something. I am out in the cold with you because (forgive the flip saying) God is where He isn't. And maybe that's where the

Church is too (when all the mitres are off and the vestments are hung up in the closet). I won't run on anymore, but I think I have said enough to make clear that I think the whole business of faith and the message of faith is in process of finding a whole new language – or of shutting up altogether. Hence the answer to your question: if God does not speak to you it is not your fault and it is not His fault, it is the fault of the whole mentality that creates the impression that He has to be constantly speaking to people. Those who are the loudest to affirm they hear Him are people not to be trusted. But nevertheless, there is a way of understanding that non-hearing is hearing. Maybe it is all too subtle.

26 OCTOBER

The crises of the age are so enormous and the mystery of evil so unfathomable: the action of well-meaning men is so absurd and tends so much to contribute to the very evils it tries to overcome: all these things should show us that the real way is prayer, and penance, and closeness to God in poverty and solitude.

27 OCTOBER

What greater thing can we have than to be empty, to be despoiled, to be orphans and exiles in this world?

28 OCTOBER

… I think what I need to learn is an almost infinite tolerance and compassion. At least this is I think my great need, because negative thought gets nowhere. I am beginning to think that in our time we will correct almost nothing, and get almost nowhere: but if we can just prepare a compassionate and receptive soil for the future, we will have done a great work.

29 OCTOBER

Certainly the love and grace of Christ are calling us together for His work, and I think it will be very fruitful. We do need much light but I am very confident that the cooperation and freedom and openness that seem promised will do wonders for us. We will all learn and all get grace to face the unexpected. It is exhilarating, isn't it?

30 OCTOBER

But there comes a time when one must see that one did nothing, one was and is a useless servant, and that this precisely is the heart of our joy in Christ Who does not estimate the value of our presumed service but only the gift of His love which makes us disappear in Him: not ontologically of course (the whole of Oriental 'pantheism' is another Western myth, because their ontology is a mystery we have not yet penetrated), but in charity.

31 OCTOBER

… Your piece on the Church in Heaven is most welcome, as it reminds me how much I need my hermitage to be peopled by the angels and saints. I need their company … And also one needs so much to look forward to the moment of arriving among them, when their joy will be increased as well as our own, and I liked especially what you said about making new friends, or rather meeting ones who had been our friends all along, and we never knew. What a day that will be.

NOVEMBER

1 NOVEMBER

The whole question of the love of God depends on whether or not you look at Him as an *object*. The more you treat Him as a 'thing', the harder it is really to love Him. But there is a difficulty about treating Him as a person, since this very soon gets to be like treating him as an imaginary person, and then sooner or later everything falls through. Hence the answer is *faith*. To love someone we have not only to know him but know him *as he is*. The only way to know God as He is, is through faith.

2 NOVEMBER

… The true reality of the Church is precisely what the Gospel said it is: the communion of 'saints' in the Holy Spirit. Let us dare to call ourselves saints because we know well enough that we are sinners and poor, and that we cannot possibly have any good that is not in and from Christ. But that in Him and from Him and with Him we have immense riches, which are, however, not our making but His gift.

3 NOVEMBER

… This is an age of deep spiritual winter, in which everything is quite cold and the leaves and birds are all gone. We have ice to walk on instead of water, but that is the only advantage. And like you I believe we should never minimize suffering and try to explain it away, especially with seemingly religious rationalizations and clichés …

4 NOVEMBER

As one spiritual man to another (if I may so speak in all humility), I speak to you from my heart of our obligation to study the truth in deep prayer and meditation, and bear witness to the light that comes from the All-Holy God into this world of darkness where He is not known and not remembered.

5 NOVEMBER

… You certainly have a vocation, but not necessarily a conventional type of vocation. … but the important thing is that you have clearly a vocation to a contemplative life, in a general way, and the only thing that needs to be found out is exactly how or where. And that is not too important because wherever you are you will be tending to the same end. … But for the rest you need to have no doubts and no fears. God is with you. … I have great confidence that everything will eventually work out well. But there is need for patience …

6 NOVEMBER

God is so much greater than all our thoughts and acts and problems and the best thing we can do is forget ourselves entirely in Him and go along where He wishes. … So let's keep praying that we will all get lost in His love. And this may help us bring more love into a world that needs it.

7 NOVEMBER

Prayers are the most important thing at the moment. And deep faith. … The psalms become more and more of a comfort, more and more full of meaning and when one realizes that they do *not* apply to the conventional situation, but to another kind of situation altogether. The psalms are for poor men, or solitary men, or men who suffer: not for liturgical enthusiasts in a comfortable, well-heated choir.

8 NOVEMBER

The basic trouble is perhaps that they [people who come to the recipient with complicated questions] are still very immature in the spiritual life, because they are very centred on a 'self' for which they want to attain the best of ends: they want to possess 'contemplation' and 'God'. But to think contemplation is something that one can 'attain' and 'possess' is just to get off on the wrong road from the very beginning. What they really need is solid and simple direction, and more than that, what they need is the kind of really basic sort of training that the Desert Fathers and the early monasteries gave: to shut up and stop all their speculation and get down to living a simple laborious life in which they forget themselves.

9 NOVEMBER

It is very very good and sweet to be always occupied with God only, and sit simply in His presence and shut up, and be healed by the mere fact that God likes to be in your soul, because you like Him to be there. And in doing this you also love your neighbour as much as you could by any action of your own: because God cannot be in your soul without that fact having an effect on other people, and not necessarily people who have ever heard of you. ...

And when I write that this is very good, I might as well write that it is bitter, too, sometimes, because it is hard to see God doing all the good that is in us, & ourselves absolutely incapable of doing anything in return.

10 NOVEMBER

Problems about the Bible often arise from our expecting the wrong things from it. It is not a manual of the spiritual life but a very mysterious record of events which are not always explained or explainable. A lot of it seems to me irrelevant, in my bad moments, especially in the Old Testament, and that is perfectly normal, I guess.

As to your problem about Christ: it comes from imposing on the Bible the demands of a non-Biblical Christology, and expanding nature. I have no explanation of how He was able to feel such dereliction, but the fact that He did so does not trouble me because it reminds me that He shared a lot of my own kind of feelings and was therefore closer to me: is closer. Each one has to work those things out in his own life, I guess. The Bible does not pretend to explain everything, and we have to be content to let a lot go without being able to figure it out logically.

11 NOVEMBER

... I think you will be able to understand what is the true way to sanctity. It is simply a way in which we lose all esteem for ourselves and find out more and more that we are nothing and that we are worth nothing, and that Jesus is everything. Souls who fail to find Him in religion are those who never learn to appreciate their own nonentity. That is something very hard to appreciate. It is impossible to feel good about being what we are. But we must take our eyes off ourselves and realize that all our joy comes from Jesus and from Him alone. Then we no longer strain our eyes trying to find some reason for rejoicing in ourselves. There is none ...

Forgetfulness of His love is the one thing that saddens Him.

12 NOVEMBER
… Unfortunately people have a mania for organisation and complication, trying to draw up detailed programmes for everything all the time, and they forget to just live.

13 NOVEMBER
Pride is crucifixion because it separates you from yourself, but to know it, & not refuse to remember it all the time, is a crucifixion that heals the separation & brings unity with yourself & with Christ, who is the centre of yourself, & with others, who are your other selves, – selves that you cannot do without.

14 NOVEMBER
Be good, keep your feet dry, your eyes open, your heart at peace and your soul in the joy of Christ. May Our Lady be with you.

15 NOVEMBER
It seems to me that a fully mystical experience has in its very essence some note of a direct spiritual *contact of two liberties*, a kind of a flash or spark which ignites an intuition [of our own inmost reality]… *plus* something much more which I can only describe as 'personal', in which God is known not as an 'object' or as 'Him up there' or 'Him in everything' nor as 'the All' but as – the biblical expression – I AM, or simply AM. But what I mean is that this is not the kind of intuition that smacks of anything procurable because it is a presence of a Person and *depends on the liberty of that Person*. And lacking the element of a free gift, a free act of love on the part of Him Who comes, the experience would lose its specifically mystical quality.

16 NOVEMBER

I know how sick you must feel of noise, and confusion, and all the rest. Perhaps, too, when this passes, you will be left slack and empty, and depressed. That too is part of the bitter gift that has been given you, and God will grant you to see the meaning of it, I am sure. Our faith demands of us that we find meaning in meaninglessness these days. It is not a source of unending comfort all the time. Those who claim that it is only tempt us against it.

17 NOVEMBER

… I am much happier with 'emptiness' when I don't have to talk about it. … As soon as I say something, then, that is 'not it' right away. Obviously the conclusion is to say nothing, and that for a great deal of the time is what I manage to do. Yet one must speak of it. Obviously, one must speak and not speak.

18 NOVEMBER

We are all nearing the end of our work. The night is falling upon us, and we find ourselves without the serenity and fulfilment that were the lot of our fathers. I do not think this is necessarily a sign that anything is lacking, but rather is to be taken as a greater incentive to trust more fully in the mercy of God, and to advance further into His mystery. Our faith can no longer serve merely as a happiness pill. It has to be the Cross and the Resurrection of Christ. And this it will be, for all of us who so desire.

19 NOVEMBER

Certainly our basic need is for truth, and not for 'images' and slogans that 'engineer consent'. We are living in a dream world. We do not know ourselves or our adversaries. We are myths to ourselves and they are myths to us.

20 NOVEMBER

Everything healthy, everything certain, everything holy, if we can find such things, they all need to be emphasized and articulated. For this it is necessary that there be communication between the hearts and minds of men, communication and not the noise of slogans or the repetition of clichés. Communication is becoming more and more difficult, and when speech is in danger of perishing or being perverted in the amplified noises of beasts, perhaps it becomes obligatory... to try to speak. There is therefore it seems to me every reason why we should attempt to cry out to one another and comfort one another, insofar as this may be possible, with the truth of Christ and also with the truth of humanism and reason. For faith cannot be preserved if reason goes under, and the Church cannot survive if man is destroyed: that is to say if his humanity is utterly debased and mechanized, while he himself remains on earth as the instrument of enormous and unidentified forces like those which press us inexorably to the brink of cataclysmic war.

21 NOVEMBER

Though 'all manner of things shall be well', we cannot help but be aware ... that we have enormous responsibilities and tasks of which we are perhaps no longer capable. Our sudden, unbalanced, top-heavy rush into technological mastery has left us without the spiritual means to face our problems. Or rather, we have thrown the spiritual means away. ... And here we all stand as prisoners of our own scientific virtuosity, ruled by immense power that we ought to be ruling and cannot. Our weapons dictate what we are to do. They force us into awful corners. They give us our living, they sustain our economy, they bolster up our politicians, they sell our mass media, in short we live by them. But if they continue to rule us we will also most surely die by them ...

22 NOVEMBER

Actually there is no question that social and communal religion tends always to be a bit formalistic. It is necessary and certainly one cannot just be completely individualistic about religion. But at the same time if one depends on the group, the parish, the monastery to do everything for one and provide all the light and inspiration and so on, then you can wait a long time before anything gets at all clear or acquires any meaning. On the other hand religion is not a matter of extraordinary spiritual experiences and that rot. The most important thing is a really simple and solid living faith. I think the thing that matters for most people is simply to live in an atmosphere of reasonable and alert faith and love for God and for other people, and in that way everything gets quite soon to have a simple religious meaning.

23 NOVEMBER

The Cross is the only way to establish peace. Until Christians come to know and understand something of the Cross, we cannot have anything but war. Unhappily the traditional Christian symbols and terminology have been exhausted by centuries of misuse and use without attention. We have lost the inner sensitivity to truth and to Christ, the fear of the Lord, without which we cannot see straight in the confusion of our world. Let us pray that Christians everywhere may recover this sensitivity ...

24 NOVEMBER

I think that part of the problem is that Anglicanism assumes a great deal and takes a lot for granted: first of all that you are able to do most of it on your own, so to speak. The Roman Church goes to the other extreme and tries to push you into everything and do it all for you, including all your thinking (and some of us don't take too kindly to this, as you may imagine). I think the best thing is to aim at the real English spirit of the *via media* with a good spirit of faith, some steady reading of the New Testament, some use of the psalms as personal prayer and some good reading and thinking about the realities of the Christian life. It is more than a matter of just getting along in a common sense pragmatic sort of way and hoping for the best, yet on the other hand we must not expect a lot of wonders and hope to see ourselves vastly improved in every way in an instant.

25 NOVEMBER
The solitary life I find very fruitful and in some ways disconcerting. It has brought me face to face with things I had never had to consider before, and I find that some pretty drastic revaluations have to be made, in my own life. This keeps me busy.

26 NOVEMBER
The basic truth is our dependence on God in a realm where so terribly much is completely unknown and in a way unknowable. What we must do is to keep that fact in mind and turn frequently to God in simple faith without expecting to 'see' Him or to understand too much about His ways, but anyway to follow the principles of the Gospel and to live for truth above all.

27 NOVEMBER
… Without contact with living examples, we soon get lost or give out. We need to be sustained in the interior work that we alone can do, with God's grace: but still there is need of the push that comes from others who do the same, and who can, in the briefest signals, communicate some of their directions to us.

28 NOVEMBER

Too many people think that the Christian conscience in social affairs needs to be expressing itself by all kinds of active demonstrations, and an infinite number of petitions and declarations. All of this is perhaps all right for those who are in the thick of such activity, though I question whether it has any real value. But for me it has and can have no value whatever.

I suppose that it will take a little time for this appearance of 'engagement' in such movements to fade away. But I am at peace in the forest here in any case, and I see more and more that there is but one thing necessary. The exterior silence of the forest makes interior silence at once imperative and easy...

29 NOVEMBER

... You should not feel too depressed by what you have had to go through. Perhaps it is not as fruitless as it may seem. ... Cheer up. Things are not as black as they may seem. Don't expect other people to understand you. Some of us do, and that is about the best one can hope for, all of us! It is a lonely business ... but we forget that God has all things in His hand and that we don't know what is happening...

30 NOVEMBER

... What matters is to do what is right whether or not it is satisfying at the moment, and to do this not out of moral obligation only but in a spirit of faith in Christ. This keeps alive in us the conviction that we are children of God for whom He has a deep and constant care, and we live in the belief that He loves us and will let nothing happen to us that is not for our good. As we go on we realize more and more how deeply this care of His for us extends into the minutest details of our lives so that He is in fact always with us and indeed in us, for we could not exist if He were not there. In this way we can develop a simple and wordless way of living in companionship with Him and this will help us to get a better realization of what our faith is all about.

DECEMBER

1 DECEMBER
The times are difficult. They call for courage and faith. Faith is in the end a lonely virtue. Lonely especially where a deeply authentic community of love is not an accomplished fact, but a job to be begun over and over …

2 DECEMBER
Anyway, we need to make straight the paths for the coming of the Consoler. And I think the Christian needs to wait with the longing and anguish of the Jew for the Messiah, not with our foregone-conclusion, accomplished-fact-that-justifies-all-our-nonsense attitude …

3 DECEMBER
Do not worry about the fact that you don't get deeply philosophical over religious things. It is better to be quite simple and have a simple faith in God and leave what you don't know to Him. … In the end, we can only say that we believe and that we don't really know.

4 DECEMBER
What is important is that the Lord comes to ask our life from us and when He asks that everything we are involved in now is completely finished, washed up, cleaned out, it is no longer seen

or heard or thought of. This life of ours should then be right in His hands all the time, not as ours but as His, a match flame we have entrusted to Him after having received it from Him in the first place. What is important is that He regards the flame as precious. Nothing else is of any account.

5 DECEMBER

Persons are known not by the intellect alone, not by principles alone, but only by love. It is when we love the other, the enemy, that we obtain from God the key to an understanding of who he is, and who we are. It is only this realisation that can open to us the real nature of our duty, and of right action.

6 DECEMBER

The Church does not consist entirely of bourgeois squares, however much some of them might want to make it appear so. ... I don't know what you want to do about it, but certainly there are other possibilities.

7 DECEMBER

For when we extend our hand to the enemy who is sinking in the abyss, God reaches out to both of us, for it is He first of all who extends our hand to the enemy. It is He who 'saves himself' in the enemy, who makes use of us to recover the lost groat which is His image in our enemy.

8 DECEMBER

What is important is the fully Christian notion of man: a notion radically modified by the mystery of the Incarnation. ... a programme of Christian culture needs to be rooted in the biblical notion of man as the object of the divine mercy, of a special concern on the part of God, as the spouse of God, as, in some mysterious sense, an epiphany of the divine wisdom.

Man in Christ. The New Adam, presupposing the Old Adam, presupposing the old paradise and the new paradise, the creation and the new creation.

9 DECEMBER
I think women are perhaps capable of salvaging something of humanity in our world today. Certainly they have a better chance of grasping and understanding and preserving a sense of Christian culture. ... The word 'wisdom' is another key word, I suspect. We are concerned not just with culture but also with wisdom, above all.

10 DECEMBER
... I will certainly keep in mind the difficulties you mention, and will pray for you. Often the best we can do is to want that which we cannot accomplish. And to trust in God, Who suffers in us in a way we do not understand. Since all that is ours is His, except sin, and even that becomes His affair when we surrender our will to Him in contrition, we can only rest in Him even when we suffer most.

11 DECEMBER
I cannot refrain from speaking to you of Abraham, and his laughter and prostration when he was told by God that he, a hundred years old, should be the father of a great nation and that from his body, almost dead, would come life to the whole world. The peak of liberty is in his laughter, which is a resurrection and a sacrament of the resurrection, the sweet and clean folly of the soul who has been liberated by God from his own nothingness. ... I wish you this laughter in any sorrow that may touch your life.

12 DECEMBER

We have to remember the terrible danger of projecting on to others all the evil we find in ourselves, so that we justify our desire to hate that evil and to destroy it in them. The basic thing in Christian ethics is to look at the *person* and not at the *nature*.

13 DECEMBER

Most of the time we only think we have problems. Because we want to have problems. Because to have problems is our way of being important somehow. It is not that we have to learn to be unimportant because we are already that. But not to refuse the privilege of being unimportant. Which is what we always do.

14 DECEMBER

Let us then, my good friend, proceed in faith, trusting in the unfailing help of God our Father and in the intercession of so great a 'cloud of witnesses', including the great monks and contemplatives of Russia ...

15 DECEMBER

And you know that whether I write or not, it makes no difference to the profound union between us in the glory of Him in Whose service we are hidden. And the lights are lit one by one outside the door of our Church, week by week. And we plunge more into the cold and the darkness. I wish I knew more about doing T'shuvah [metanoia or penance]. It is the only thing that seems to make much sense in these days. And in the political dark I light small, frail lights about peace and hold them up in the whirlwind.

16 DECEMBER

That we should 'love God' not merely to convince ourselves that we are good people, or to get a warm glow of peace, or to fit in with an approving group, or to get rid of anxiety, but to throw all that to the winds, and anxiety or not, even though we realize the utter depth of our inadequacy, to realize that this simply does not matter in the 'eyes of God' for, as we are, with our misfortunes and needs, 'we are His joy' and He delights to be loved by us with perfect confidence in Him because He is love itself.

17 DECEMBER

Surely we ought to see now that repentance means something far deeper than we have suspected: it can no longer be a matter of setting things right according to the norms of our own small group, the immediate society in which we live. We have to open our hearts to a universal and all-embracing love that knows no limits and no obstacles, a love that is not scandalised by the sinner, a love that takes upon itself the sins of the world. There must be total love of all, even of the most distant, even of the most hostile.

18 DECEMBER

It is not that we have to sweat and groan to placate an austere Father God in our own imagination, but rather to realize, with liberation and joy, that *He is not that at all*. That in fact He is none of our idols, none of our figments, nothing that we can imagine anyway, but that He is Love Itself. And if we realize this and love Him simply and purely in order to 'please Him', we become as it were His 'crown' and His 'delight' and life itself is transformed in this light which is disinterested love.

19 DECEMBER

Christ the Lord is the Word Who has assumed our nature, which is one in all of us. He has perfectly fulfilled and so to speak transfigured and elevated not only nature but the natural law which is, in its most basic expression, treating our brother as one who has the same nature as we have.

20 DECEMBER

I know that as one grows older life tends to get a little lonely sometimes, but we have to look at that in the right way: it can bring us closer to God who is our best friend. So trust in the Sacred Heart and stay with Him and the Blessed Mother. You will find they will give you much comfort and strength and prepare you to see them face to face.

21 DECEMBER

Do not let yourself be disturbed too much by either friends or enemies. ... May you find again within yourself the deep life-giving silence which is genuine truth and the source of truth: for it is a fountain of life and a window into the abyss of eternity and God. ... it is an inviolable house of peace, a fortress in the depths of our being, the virginity of our soul where, like the Blessed Mary, we give our brave and humble answer to life, the 'Yes' which brings Christ into the world.

22 DECEMBER

...We must seek Him and not ourselves. That is to say we must not seek some special experience or 'state' but only God, and accept whatever He may will for us. In our prayer we should avoid everything that makes us uselessly examine and analyze ourselves, and simply go to Him in faith, even if it means that we have to be very patient with a form of prayer that seems dark and arid. He will teach us if we are patient and trust in Him.

23 DECEMBER

Christmas, then, is not just a sweet regression to breast-feeding and infancy. It is a serious and sometimes difficult feast. Difficult especially if, for psychological reasons, we fail to grasp the indestructible kernel of hope that is in it. If we are just looking for a little consolation – we may be disappointed. Let us pray for one another, love one another in truth, in the sobriety of earnest, Christian hope: for hope, says Paul, does not deceive. A blessed and joyous Christmas to all of you.

24 DECEMBER

… I will feast with you spiritually in the light of the Child of God Who comes shyly and silently into the midst of our darkness and transforms the winter night into Paradise for those who, like the Shepherds and the humble Kings, come to find Him where no one thinks of looking: in the obviousness and poverty of … ordinary everyday life.

25 DECEMBER

All best wishes always, and every blessing in this holy season when the animals and the shepherds show us the way back to our child mind and to Him in Whom is hidden our original face before we are born. Be of good cheer. They cannot silence either Chuang Tzu or this Child, in China or anywhere. They will be heard in the middle of the night saying nothing and everybody will come to their senses.

26 DECEMBER

The question of detachment depends it seems to me first of all on self-knowledge. Or rather the two are mutually interdependent. One must know what are the real attachments in his soul before he can effectively work against them, and one must have a detached will in order to see the truth of one's attachments. In practice, the events of life bring us face to face, in painful situations, with the places in which we are attached to our inner egoism. Exterior detachment is easier: it is a matter of renouncing comforts and gratifications of the sensual appetites, and this renunciation is of course essential. ... But inner detachment centres around the 'self', especially in one's pride, one's desire to react and to defend or to assert 'self' in one's own will. ... I think it is necessary for us to see that God Himself works to purify us of this inner 'self' that tends to resist Him and to assert itself against Him. Our faith must teach us to see His will and to bend to His will precisely in those points where He attacks the self, even through the actions of other people. Here the unjust and unkind actions of others, even though objectionable in themselves, can help us to strip ourselves of interior attachment.

27 DECEMBER

Of course there are trials, but there is also the grace of God with which to bear them, and the assurance that all is worthwhile. You certainly see life and death in a new light, living alone. In social life, there is a great deal that has been unconsciously built in to protect man from the fear of death.

28 DECEMBER

... I will keep you all in my prayers... . And the best thing I can tell you is, value your contemplative vocation; prize it above everything, don't let anyone talk you out of it, and don't let anyone steer you away from solitude as long as it is God's will for you … Keep me in your good prayers.

29 DECEMBER

The Lord knows what He intends to do for your soul … Do not be discouraged. If you can bear this patiently you will do great good for yourself and for others. I know it must be awfully hard and lonely. But there is no other way to heaven than the way of hardship and loneliness. It was lonely for the Christ Child to be born in a stable. And He did not have many friends around Him when He was on the Cross. Bear with the misunderstandings that come your way. People are nervous and their nerves are sick, sometimes it is not their fault if they seem to be hard on us.

30 DECEMBER

All best Christmas wishes and warm blessings for the new year. May Our Lord come to us in peace and in simplicity, and increase our faith and love for Him. And may this poor world have peace, somehow, in spite of the madness and absurdity of men and weapons. For now it is the weapons themselves that make all the decisions: men humbly obey the creations of their own technology. I wonder if a few of us may persuade our fellows to retain at least enough freedom to use machines instead of being used by them.

31 DECEMBER

Realize, then, that you are loved. And open your heart to that love, and even if the world collapses around you, do not let anything turn you aside from loving and praising God. We have been saved and Redeemed by the Precious Blood of Jesus, and there is no room for sadness or doubt in our lives, no room for preoccupation with our faults and miseries. We must not only trust, but we must go forward and make our lives fruitful with the offering of our own love: our giving of ourselves in a positive creation, a living of a new life in a new world, in a new dimension.

GLOSSARY

epectasis: a theological term [often spelt epektasis] attributed to St Gregory of Nyssa to refer to the drawing of the soul ever onwards towards God without end and through eternity. In Philippians 3: 13–14, St Paul describes his journey of stretching and straining forward [epekteinomenos] a constant moving forward in an attempt to grasp something. Thomas Merton writes, 'As to epectasis: I do not consider it a 'state' at all but so to speak a basic law of the spiritual life.' (Taken from a letter to Etta Gullick, 31 August 1962, in *The Hidden Ground of Love*, p. 354)

fana (Sufi): meaning 'annihilation'. It is sometimes used in conjunction with the term baqa meaning 'reintegration'. In his notes for a paper due to be delivered at Calcutta on October 1968 on Monastic Experience and East–West Dialogue Merton writes of a 'certain universality and wholeness. ...Transcending the limits that separate subject from object and self from not-self, this development achieves a wholeness which is described in various ways by the different religions: a self-realization of atman, of Void, of life in Christ, of fana and baqa (annihilation and reintegration according to Sufism), etc.' (Thomas Merton, *The Asian Journal of Thomas Merton*, London: Sheldon Press, 1974, p. 310)

prajna (Sanskrit): in Buddhism, supreme knowledge or wisdom; spiritual awakening; wisdom which brings liberation. (Thomas Merton, *The Asian Journal of Thomas Merton*, London: Sheldon Press, 1974, p. 393)

satori (Japanese): in Zen Buddhism, awakening, illumination, enlightenment; the state of consciousness held to be comparable to that special level of insight attained by the Buddha while seated in meditation under the sacred Tree of Enlightenment in the sixth century BC. (Thomas Merton, *The Other Side of the Mountain, The Journals of Thomas Merton, Volume 7 1967–1968*, Edited by Patrick Hart OCSO, San Francisco: HarperSanFrancisco, 1998, p. 334)

sobornost (Russian Orthodox): Thomas Merton writes, 'I am very drawn to the Russian idea of *sobornost* [the doctrine of the Spirit acting and leading the whole Church into the truth] which seems to me to be essential to the notion of the Church, in some form or other'. (Taken from a letter to Sergius Bolshakoff, 11 November 1963, in *The Hidden Ground of Love*, p. 104)

NOTES

PREFACE

1. Thomas Merton, *The Hidden Ground of Love* p. 384
2. Dr Paul M. Pearson (personal communication 12 June 2011)
3. *Compassionate Fire, The Letters of Thomas Merton and Catherine de Hueck Doherty* edited by Robert A. Wild (Notre Dame, Indiana: Ave Maria Press, 2009, p. 54)
4. Ibid. p. 14
5. Foreword by Mother Rosemary SLG to *Loving God Whatever: Through the Year with Sister Jane* edited by Jim Cotter and Sister Avis Mary SLG (Oxford: SLG Press Fairacres Publications, 2006, 155 p. vii)
6. 'Lectio Divina' 5 (unpublished, undated, archives of the Thomas Merton Center, Louisville, Kentucky quoted in *The Thomas Merton Encyclopedia* by William H. Shannon, Christine M. Bochen and Patrick F. O'Connell (Maryknoll, New York: Orbis Books, 2002, p. 254)

REFERENCES

The extracts are taken from the following volumes of letters:

The Hidden Ground of Love: The Letters of Thomas Merton on Religious Experience and Social Concerns. Selected and edited by William H. Shannon (London: Collins Flame, 1985) referenced below as *HG of L*.

The Road to Joy: The Letters of Thomas Merton to New and Old Friends. Selected and edited by Robert E. Daggy (London: Collins Flame, 1989) referenced below as *R to J*.

The School of Charity: The Letters of Thomas Merton on Religious Renewal and Spiritual Direction. Selected and edited by Brother Patrick Hart (San Diego, New York and London: Harcourt Brace Jovanovich, 1990) referenced below as *S of C*.

The Courage for Truth: The Letters of Thomas Merton to Writers. Selected and edited by Christine M. Bochen (San Diego, New York and London: Harcourt Brace & Company, 1993) referenced below as *C for T*.

Witness to Freedom: The Letters of Thomas Merton in Times of Crisis. Selected and edited by William H. Shannon (New York: Farrar, Straus & Giroux, 1994) referenced below as *W to F*.

JANUARY

1 To Jim Frost, 7 January 1964, *R to J*, p. 330
2 To Linda (Parsons) Sabbath, 29 January 1966, *HG of L*, p. 525
3 To Linda (Parsons) Sabbath, 13 January 1966, *HG of L*, p. 523
4 To Victoria Ocampo, 13 January 1963, *C for T*, p. 209
5 To Victoria Ocampo, 20 January 1967, *C for T*, p. 210
6 To Archimandrite Sophrony, 26 January 1961, *HG of L*, p. 560
7 To Dame B., 30 January 1966, *S of C*, p. 297
8 To Father G., 7 January 1967, *S of C*, p. 326
9 To Abdul Aziz, 2 January 1966, *HG of L*, p. 63
10 To Father Chrysogonus Waddell, 4 January 1964, *S of C*, p. 191
11 To an Unidentified Friend, 9 January 1967, *R to J*, p. 345
12 To Catherine de Hueck Doherty, 12 January 1966, *HG of L*, p. 22
13 To Linda (Parsons) Sabbath, 13 January 1966, *HG of L*, p. 523
14 To Catherine de Hueck Doherty, 12 January 1966, *HG of L*, p. 24
15 To Mother Coakley RSCJ, 3 January 1965, *S of C*, p. 261
16 To Dona Luisa Coomaraswamy, 13 January 1961, *HG of L*, p. 127
17 To Abdul Aziz, 2 January 1966, *HG of L*, p. 64
18 To Zalman Schachter, 11 January 1963, *HG of L*, p. 537
19 To Dame Marcella Van Bruyn, 2 January 1964, *S of C*, p. 191
20 To Pablo Antonio Cuadra, 4 January 1960, *C for T*, p. 188
21 To Catherine de Hueck Doherty, 12 January 1966, *HG of L*, p. 23

22 To Dona Luisa Coomaraswamy, 13 January 1961, *HG of L*, p. 126

23 To Abdul Aziz, 16 January 1968, *HG of L*, p. 66

24 To Zalman Schachter, 18 January 1961, *HG of L*, p. 533

25 To Zalman Schachter, 18 January 1961, *HG of L*, p. 533

26 To Etta Gullick, 18 January 1963, *HG of L*, p. 357

27 To Etta Gullick, 18 January 1963, *HG of L*, p. 357

28 To Archimandrite Sophrony, 26 January 1961, *HG of L*, p. 559

29 To Father Peter Minard OSB, 9 January 1965, *S of C*, p. 263

30 To Archimandrite Sophrony, 26 January 1961, *HG of L*, p. 559

31 To Louis Massignon, 29 October 1960, *W to F*, p. 279

FEBRUARY

1 To Linda (Parsons) Sabbath, 29 January 1966, *HG of L*, p. 525

2 To Zalman Schachter, 7 April 1964, *HG of L*, p. 539

3 To Etta Gullick, 29 January 1962, *HG of L*, p. 350

4 To Linda (Parsons) Sabbath, 29 January 1966, *HG of L*, p. 526

5 To Beatrice Olmstead and family, 6 February 1960, *R to J*, p. 274

6 To Tashi Tshering, February 1962, *R to J*, p. 320

7 To Linda (Parsons) Sabbath, 29 January 1966, *HG of L*, p. 525

8 To James Forest, 29 January 1962, *HG of L*, p. 263

9 To Dame B., 30 January 1966, *S of C*, p. 297

10 To Dame B., 30 January 1966, *S of C*, p. 297

11 To James Forest, 29 January 1962, *HG of L*, p. 262

12 To Dorothy Day, 9 February 1967, *HG of L*, p. 152

13 Circular letter to friends, Lent 1967, *R to J*, p. 99

14 To Dorothy Day, 4 February 1960, *HG of L*, p. 137
15 To Dom Gabriel Sortais, 12 February 1953, *S of C*, p. 52
16 To Linda (Parsons) Sabbath, 12 February 1966, *HG of L*, p. 526
17 To John C. H. Wu, 31 January 1965, *HG of L*, p. 627
18 To Linda (Parsons) Sabbath, 12 February 1966, *HG of L*, p. 527
19 To John Harris, 31 January 1959, *HG of L*, p. 387
20 To W. H. Ferry, 17 February 1962, *HG of L*, p. 208
21 To James Forest, 21 February 1966, *HG of L*, p. 294
22 To S.S. (Rabbi Steven Schwarzschild), 24 February 1962, *W to F*, p. 35
23 To Daniel J. Berrigan, 23 February 1964, *HG of L*, p. 81
24 To Dona Luisa Coomaraswamy, 12 February 1961, *HG of L*, p. 129
25 To Jacques Maritain, 22 February 1960, *C for T*, p. 29
26 To Sister Anita (Ann) Wasserman OCD, 25 February 1953, *W to F*, p. 180
27 Circular letter to friends, Septuagesima Sunday 1967, *R to J*, p. 96
28 To James Forest, 21 February 1966, *HG of L*, p. 297
29 To James Forest, 21 February 1966, *HG of L*, p. 296

MARCH
1 To Brother Frances Taparra OCSO, 2 March 1964, *S of C*, p. 208
2 To Naomi Burton Stone, 3 March 1956, *W to F*, p. 132
3 To Mother Myriam Dardenne, 6 March 1965, *S of C*, p. 268
4 To Mother Neri RSCJ, 6 March 1968, *S of C*, p. 369
5 To Rosemary Radford Ruether, 9 March 1967, *HG of L*, p. 503
6 To Zalman Schachter, 15 February 1962, *HG of L*, p. 535

7 To Sister K., 10 March 1967, *S of C*, p. 329

8 To Rosemary Radford Ruether, 9 March 1967, *HG of L*, p. 502

9 To Sister K., 10 March 1967, *S of C*, p. 329

10 To Marco Pallis, 10 March 1965, *HG of L*, p. 468

11 To Sister K., 10 March 1967, *S of C*, p. 330

12 To Robert Lawrence Williams, 10 March 1965, *HG of L*, p. 594

13 To Ernesto Cardenal, 11 March 1967, *C for T*, p. 159

14 To Daisetz T. Suzuki, 12 March 1959, *HG of L*, p. 561

15 To Ernesto Cardenal, 11 March 1961, *C for T*, p. 124

16 To José Coronel Urtecho, 15 March 1964, *C for T*, p. 172

17 To Czeslaw Milosz, 15 March 1968, *C for T*, p. 85

18 To Mother M. L. Schroen, 17 March 1966, *S of C*, p. 301

19 To Rosemary Radford Ruether, 19 March 1967, *HG of L*, p. 508

20 To Mother M. L. Schroen, 17 March 1966, *S of C*, p. 302

21 To Linda (Parsons) Sabbath, 19 March 1966, *HG of L*, p. 527

22 To Jeanette Yakel, 21 March 1967, *R to J*, p. 347

23 To James Forest, 21 March 1967, *HG of L*, p. 302

24 To Etta Gullick, 24 March 1963, *HG of L*, p. 358

25 To Linda (Parsons) Sabbath, 19 March 1966, *HG of L*, p. 527

26 To Victor Hammer, 14 May 1959, *W to F*, p. 4

27 To Linda (Parsons) Sabbath, 19 March 1966, *HG of L*, p. 528

28 To Linda (Parsons) Sabbath, 19 March 1966, *HG of L*, p. 528

29 To Sister L., 31 March 1960, *S of C*, p. 129

30 To Mark Van Doren, 9 August 1962, *R to J*, p. 45

31 To Mark Van Doren, 24 February 1966, *R to J*, p. 50

APRIL

1 Circular letter to friends, Easter 1967, *R to J*, p. 102

2 To Dorothy Day, 9 April 1962, *HG of L*, p. 145

3 To Abdul Aziz, 30 January 1961, *HG of L*, p. 47

4 To John C. H. Wu, 1 April 1961, *HG of L*, p. 614

5 Circular letter to friends, Easter 1967, *R to J*, p. 101

6 To Czeslaw Milosz, 28 February 1959, *C for T*, p. 57

7 To John J. Wright, 20 February 1964, *HG of L*, p. 609

8 To Father Brendan Connelly, 3 April 1965, *S of C*, p. 271

9 To Abdul Aziz, 4 April 1962, *HG of L*, p. 52

10 To Richard Bass, 5 April 1965, *W to F*, p. 320

11 To Catherine de Hueck Doherty, 14 February 1949, *HG of L*, p. 12

12 To Sister M., 9 April 1968, *S of C*, p. 375

13 To Ludovico Silva, 10 April 1965, *C for T*, p. 225

14 To William Robert Miller, 10 April 1965, *W to F*, p. 251

15 To Daisetz T. Suzuki, 11 April 1959, *HG of L*, p. 564

16 To Linda (Parsons) Sabbath, 12 February 1966, *HG of L*, p. 526

17 To Daisetz T. Suzuki, 11 April 1959, *HG of L*, p. 563

18 To Daisetz T. Suzuki, 11 April 1959, *HG of L*, p. 563

19 To John C. H. Wu, 11 April 1961, *HG of L*, p. 615

20 To Etta Gullick, 29 April 1963, *HG of L*, p. 359

21 To June J. Yungblut, 29 March 1968, *HG of L*, p. 642

22 To Sister Anita (Ann) Wasserman OCD, 30 April 1957, *W to F*, p. 185

23 To Amiya Chakravarty, 13 April 1967, *HG of L*, p. 115

24 To Agnes Smith, 28 April 1968, *W to F*, p. 340

25 To Etta Gullick, 26 April 1968, *HG of L*, p. 379

26 To Joseph Tjo Tchel-oung, 28 April 1961, *R to J*, p. 319

27 To Sergius Bolshakoff, 26 April 1968, *HG of L*, p. 107

28 To an English Carmelite Prioress, 22 April 1965, *S of C*, p. 274

REFERENCES

29 To Mother C., 14 April 1968, *S of C*, p. 377
30 To Amiya Chakravarty, 13 April 1967, *HG of L*, p. 115

MAY

1 To Linda (Parsons) Sabbath, 19 March 1966, *HG of L*, p. 527
2 To a Woman Religious, 27 March 1968, *W to F*, p. 197
3 To Robert Lax May 1947, *R to J*, p. 169
4 To Robert Lawrence Williams, 1 May 1967, *HG of L*, p. 601
5 To Daisetz T. Suzuki, 3 May 1965, *HG of L*, p. 571
6 To Daisetz T. Suzuki, 11 April 1959, *HG of L*, p. 565
7 To Amiya Chakravarty, 13 April 1967, *HG of L*, p. 116
8 To Czeslaw Milosz, 28 March 1961, *C for T*, p. 73
9 To June J. Yungblut, 29 March 1968, *HG of L*, p. 644
10 To Mark Van Doren, 3 July 1956, *R to J*, p. 29
11 To Catherine de Hueck Doherty, 14 February 1949, *HG of L*, p. 12
12 To Daisetz T. Suzuki, 3 May 1965, *HG of L*, p. 570
13 To Sister Anita (Ann) Wasserman OCD, 3 May 1952, *W to F*, p. 178
14 To John Harris, 5 May 1959, *HG of L*, p. 388
15 To Amiya Chakravarty, 13 April 1967, *HG of L*, p. 115
16 To Joseph Tjo Tchel-oung, 28 April 1961, *R to J*, p. 319
17 To Mark Van Doren, 3 July 1956, *R to J*, p. 29
18 To John Harris, 5 May 1959, *HG of L*, p. 390
19 To Gabrielle Mueller, 10 May 1965, *W to F*, p. 321
20 To Miguel Grinberg, 11 May 1964, *C for T*, p. 198
21 To Mark Van Doren, 16 February 1961, *R to J*, p. 40
22 To John Harris, 5 May 1959, *HG of L*, p. 390
23 To Sister Anita (Ann) Wasserman OCD, 8 May 1954, *W to F*, p. 182
24 To Paul Sih, 9 May 1962, *HG of L*, p. 551

25 To Mark Van Doren, 11 February 1964, *R to J*, p. 47
26 To Dom Jean Leclercq, 11 May 1965, *S of C*, p. 280
27 To Victor Hammer, 14 May 1959, *W to F*, p. 5
28 Circular letter to friends, Pentecost 1967, *R to J*, p. 102
29 To Abdul Aziz, 13 May 1961, *HG of L*, p. 49
30 To Linda (Parsons) Sabbath, 14 May 1966, *HG of L*, p. 529
31 To Victor Hammer, 14 May 1959, *W to F*, p. 5

JUNE
1 To Mark Van Doren, 6 June 1959, *R to J*, p. 34
2 To Evora Arca de Sardinia, 15 May 1961, *W to F*, p. 77
3 To Ernesto Cardenal, 16 May 1962, *C for T*, p. 132
4 To Mark Van Doren, 30 March 1948, *R to J*, p. 22
5 To Miguel Grinberg, 11 May 1964, *C for T*, p. 198
6 To John C. H. Wu, 19 May 1961, *HG of L*, p. 617
7 To Czeslaw Milosz, 21 May 1959, *C for T*, p. 59
8 To G. M. (probably Gwen Myers), *c*. June 1962, *W to F*, p. 57
9 To V. D. (Valerie Delacorte), early June 1962, *W to F*, p. 52
10 To Sister Marialein Lorenz's Class, 2 June 1949, *R to J*, p. 317
11 To Sister Marialein Lorenz's Class, 2 June 1949, *R to J*, p. 316
12 To Czeslaw Milosz, 21 May 1959, *C for T*, p. 60
13 To Sister Marialein Lorenz's Class, 2 June 1949, *R to J*, p. 316
14 To Catherine de Hueck Doherty, 4 June 1962, *HG of L*, p. 19
15 To Sister A., 21 May 1953, *S of C*, p. 62
16 To Catherine de Hueck Doherty, 4 June 1962, *HG of L*, p. 19
17 To Sister A., 21 May 1953, *S of C*, p. 61

18 To Catherine de Hueck Doherty, 4 June 1962, *HG of L*, p. 19

19 To Linda (Parsons) Sabbath, 26 May 1966, *HG of L*, p. 529

20 To Mother O., 31 May 1967, *S of C*, p. 334

21 Circular letter to friends, Midsummer 1967, *R to J*, p. 106

22 To Sister A., 21 May 1953, *S of C*, p. 61

23 To Catherine de Hueck Doherty, 4 June 1962, *HG of L*, p. 19

24 To Naomi Burton Stone, 4 June 1956, *W to F*, p. 138

25 To Sister A., 21 May 1953, *S of C*, p. 60

26 To Mother O., 31 May 1967, *S of C*, p. 333

27 To Herbert Mason, 6 June 1959, *W to F*, p. 262

28 To John Harris, 8 June 1962, *HG of L*, p. 398

29 To Jacques Maritain, 11 June 1963, *C for T*, p. 38

30 To Jeanne Burdick, 11 June 1962, *HG of L*, p. 110

JULY

1   To Marco Pallis, 17 June 1965, *HG of L*, p. 471

2   To Linda (Parsons) Sabbath, 18 June 1966, *HG of L*, p. 530

3   To Dame Marcella Van Bruyn, 16 June 1965, *S of C*, p. 285

4   To Sister Elaine M. Bane OSF, 4 July 1962, *S of C*, p. 145

5   To Dom Jean Leclercq, 5 July 1965, *S of C*, p. 286

6   To Linda (Parsons) Sabbath, 18 June 1966, *HG of L*, p. 529

7   To Mrs. Leonard, 20 June 1959, *W to F*, p. 301

8   To William Johnston, 5 July 1967, *HG of L*, p. 443

9   To Margaret Randall, 6 July 1967, *C for T*, p. 221

10 To Miguel Grinberg, 21 June 1963, *C for T*, p. 197

11 To Dom Jean Leclercq, 7 July 1966, *S of C*, p. 309

12 To Dorothy Day, 9 July 1959, *HG of L*, p. 136

13 To Mr. Wainwright, 10 July 1965, *W to F*, p. 254

14 To John Harris, 22 June 1959, *HG of L*, p. 392

15 To John Harris, 22 June 1959, *HG of L*, p. 392

16 To Father Thomas Fidelis (Francis) Smith OCSO, 29 June 1963, *S of C*, p. 177

17 To Abdul Aziz, 28 June 1964, *HG of L*, p. 58

18 To José Coronel Urtecho, 30 June 1965, *C for T*, p. 175

19 To Abdul Aziz, 28 June 1964, *HG of L*, p. 59

20 To Mother Myriam Dardenne, 20 July 1968, *S of C*, p. 391

21 To Louis Massignon, 20 July 1960, *W to F*, p. 278

22 To Catherine de Hueck Doherty, 22 July 1961, *HG of L*, p. 18

23 To Catherine de Hueck Doherty, 22 July 1961, *HG of L*, p. 18

24 To 'John', 24 July 1963, *R to J*, p. 328

25 To Marco Pallis, 17 June 1965, *HG of L*, p. 471

26 To John Harris, 8 June 1962, *HG of L*, p. 398

27 To Dom Pierre Van der Meer OSB, 28 July 1961, *S of C*, p. 139

28 To Sister M. Emmanuel, 28 July 1960, *HG of L*, p. 184

29 To Etta Gullick, 28 July 1963, *HG of L*, p. 361

30 To Etta Gullick, 28 July 1963, *HG of L*, p. 362

31 To Daniel J. Berrigan, 4 August 1964, *HG of L*, p. 84

AUGUST

1   To Pablo Antonio Cuadra, 1 August 1963, *C for T*, p. 191

2   To Cintio Vitier, 1 August 1963, *C for T*, p. 237

3   To Etta Gullick, 1 August 1966, *HG of L*, p. 376

4   To Lawrence Ferlinghetti, 2 August 1961, *C for T*, p. 269

5   To Daniel J. Berrigan, 4 August 1964, *HG of L*, p. 83

6   To Mother Myriam Dardenne, 5 August 1968, *S of C*, p. 393

7   To Linda (Parsons) Sabbath, 7 August 1967, *HG of L*, p. 532

8   To Dom Gabriel Sortais, 13 August 1953, *S of C*, p. 65

9   To Dorothy Day, 17 August 1960, *HG of L*, p. 138

10 To Catherine de Hueck Doherty, 22 August 1956, *HG of L*, p. 14

11 To Dorothy Day, 17 August 1960, *HG of L*, p. 138

12 To Jacques Maritain, 17 August 1960, *C for T*, p. 32

13 To Jacques Maritain, 18 December 1960, *C for T*, p. 33

14 To Dorothy Day, 18 August 1967, *HG of L*, p. 152

15 To Dom Francis Decroix, 21 August 1967, *HG of L*, p. 157

16 To Catherine de Hueck Doherty, 22 August 1956, *HG of L*, p. 13

17 To Dom Francis Decroix, 22 August 1967, *HG of L*, p. 159

18 To Catherine de Hueck Doherty, 22 August 1956, *HG of L*, p. 13

19 To Dom Francis Decroix, 21 August 1967, *HG of L*, p. 158

20 To Catherine de Hueck Doherty, 22 August 1956, *HG of L*, p. 14

21 To Boris Pasternak, 22 August 1958, *C for T*, p. 88

22 To Dom Francis Decroix, 21 August 1967, *HG of L*, p. 156

23 To Catherine de Hueck Doherty, 22 August 1956, *HG of L*, p. 14

24 To Pablo Antonio Cuadra, 22 August 1959, *C for T*, p. 187

25 To Herbert Mason, 24 August 1959, *W to F*, p. 263

26 To Jacques Maritain, 10 October 1960, *C for T*, p. 33

27 To Sister Therese Lentfoehr SDS, 28 August 1949, *R to J*, p. 195

28 To Dom Francis Decroix, 21 August 1967, *HG of L*, p. 156

29 To Sister Therese Lentfoehr SDS, 28 August 1949, *R to J*, p. 195

30 To Dom Jacques Winandy, 30 August 1965, *S of C*, p. 290

31 To Etta Gullick, 31 August 1962, *HG of L*, p. 354

SEPTEMBER

1 To Dom Gabriel Sortais, 1 September 1956, *S of C*, p. 98
2 To Dom Francis Decroix, 21 August 1967, *HG of L*, p. 156
3 To Alfonso Cortés, 3 September 1965, *C for T*, p. 177
4 To Dom Francis Decroix, 21 August 1967, *HG of L*, p. 157
5 To Helen Wolff, 5 September 1960, *C for T*, p. 103
6 To Robert Lawrence Williams, 5 September 1967, *HG of L*, p. 602
7 To Mother Myriam Dardenne, 7 September 1968, *S of C*, p. 396
8 To Etta Gullick, 9 September 1961, *HG of L*, p. 346
9 To Mother Myriam Dardenne, 7 September 1968, *S of C*, p. 396
10 To Mother Myriam Dardenne, 7 September 1968, *S of C*, p. 397
11 To E.I. Watkin, 11 September 1962, *HG of L*, p. 579
12 To Czeslaw Milosz, 12 September 1959, *C for T*, p. 64
13 To Czeslaw Milosz, 12 September 1959, *C for T*, p. 62
14 To Mother Myriam Dardenne, 7 September 1968, *S of C*, p. 396
15 To John Harris, 12 September 1959, *HG of L*, p. 393
16 To Christopher Mwoleka, 13 September 1967, *HG of L*, p. 462
17 To Mother Angela Collins OCD, 16 September 1960, *S of C*, p. 134
18 To Sister Miriam Benedict OSB, 16 September 1967, *S of C*, p. 347
19 To Sister Therese Lentfoehr SDS, 17 September 1964, *R to J*, p. 249
20 To Dorothy Day, 19 September 1967, *HG of L*, p. 153
21 To Catherine de Hueck Doherty, 18 September 1958, *HG of L*, p. 17
22 To Evelyn Waugh, 22 September 1948, *C for T*, p. 9

23 To Catherine de Hueck Doherty, 18 September 1958, *HG of L*, p. 17

24 To Catherine de Hueck Doherty, 18 September 1958, *HG of L*, p. 16

25 To Dona Luisa Coomaraswamy, 24 September 1961, *HG of L*, p. 133

26 To Father Aelred Squire, 25 September 1967, *S of C*, p. 349

27 To Dona Luisa Coomaraswamy, 24 September 1961, *HG of L*, p. 132

28 To Father Aelred Squire, 25 September 1967, *S of C*, p. 349

29 To Dona Luisa Coomaraswamy, 24 September 1961, *HG of L*, p. 133

30 To Dona Luisa Coomaraswamy, 24 September 1961, *HG of L*, p. 132

OCTOBER

1 To Etta Gullick, 9 September 1961, *HG of L*, p. 346

2 To Abbot James Fox, 1 October 1949, *S of C*, p. 17

3 To Father Bruno Scott James, 1 October 1960, *S of C*, p. 137

4 To a Woman Religious Superior, 1 October 1960, *W to F*, p. 193

5 To Marco Pallis, 4 October 1963, *HG of L*, p. 466

6 To Father Bruno Scott James, 1 October 1960, *S of C*, p. 138

7 To Linda (Parsons) Sabbath, 4 October 1965, *HG of L*, p. 520

8 To Father Bruno Scott James, 1 October 1960, *S of C*, p. 137

9 To E.I. Watkin, 15 November 1962, *HG of L*, p. 580

10 To Catherine de Hueck Doherty, 6 October 1941, *HG of L*, p. 6

11 To Daniel J. Berrigan, 10 October 1967, *HG of L*, p. 98

12 To Mr Omloo, 12 October 1965, *W to F*, p. 323

13 To Pablo Antonio Cuadra, 13 October 1958, *C for T*, p. 181

14 To Abbot Flavian Burns, 20 October 1968, *S of C*, p. 404

15 To Ernesto Cardenal, 24 October 1959, *C for T*, p. 117

16 To Daisetz T. Suzuki, 24 October 1959, *HG of L*, p. 568

17 To Sergius Bolshakoff, 28 October 1964, *HG of L*, p. 105

18 To Etta Gullick, 29 October 1962, *HG of L*, p. 355

19 To Louis Massignon, 29 October 1960, *W to F*, p. 280

20 To Robert Lawrence Williams, 30 October 1964, *HG of L*, p. 591

21 To Susie, 1 November 1965, *W to F*, p. 324

22 To Sister Anita (Ann) Wasserman OCD, 6 November 1953, *W to F*, p. 181

23 To Abdul Aziz, 7 November 1965, *HG of L*, p. 61

24 To Katharine Champney, 10 November 1966, *W to F*, p. 327

25 To Katharine Champney, 10 November 1966, *W to F*, p. 329

26 To Catherine de Hueck Doherty, 12 November 1962, *HG of L*, p. 20

27 To Etienne Gilson, 12 November 1951, *S of C*, p. 31

28 To Catherine de Hueck Doherty, 12 November 1962, *HG of L*, p. 20

29 To Sister Elaine M. Bane, 14 November 1967, *S of C*, p. 353

30 To E.I. Watkin, 15 November 1962, *HG of L*, p. 580

31 To Jacques Maritain, 6 October 1965, *C for T*, p. 47

NOVEMBER
1 To a Gethsemani Brother, 15 November (no year), *W to F*, p. 243

2 To E.I. Watkin, 15 November 1962, *HG of L*, p. 580

3 To Helen Wolff, 16 November 1959, *C for T*, p. 99

4 To Abdul Aziz, 17 November 1960, *HG of L*, p. 45

5 To Ernesto Cardenal, 18 November 1959, *C for T*, p. 119

6 To Mother Coakley, 16 November 1966, *S of C*, p. 321

7 To Ernesto Cardenal, 18 November 1959, *C for T*, p. 120

8 To Catherine de Hueck Doherty, 21 November 1964, *HG of L*, p. 22

9 To Robert Lax, 21 November 1942, *R to J*, p. 164

10 To Tim Scimeca, 11 July 1967, *W to F*, p. 334

11 To Sister Anita (Ann) Wasserman OCD, 21 November 1952, *W to F*, p. 178

12 To Catherine de Hueck Doherty, 21 November 1964, *HG of L*, p. 22

13 To Robert Lax, 23 November 1943, *R to J*, p. 167

14 To Father Tarcisius (James) Conner OCSO, 27 November 1962, *S of C*, p. 158

15 To Aldous Huxley, 27 November 1958, *HG of L*, p. 438

16 To Jacqueline Kennedy, 27 November 1963, *HG of L*, p. 450

17 To Daisetz T. Suzuki, 30 November 1959, *HG of L*, p. 569

18 To Alceu Amoroso Lima, November 1961, *C for T*, p. 166

19 To Ethel Kennedy, December 1961, *HG of L*, p. 446

20 To Alceu Amoroso Lima, November 1961, *C for T*, p. 165

21 To C.L. (Clare Boothe Luce), December 1961 or January 1962, *W to F*, p. 26

22 To Agnes Gertrude Stonehewer Merton [Aunt Kit], 27 May 1964, *R to J*, p. 62

23 To John C. Heidbrink, 2 December 1961, *HG of L*, p. 405

24 To Agnes Gertrude Stonehewer Merton [Aunt Kit], 27 May 1964, *R to J*, p. 62

25 To Abraham Heschel, 6 December 1965, *HG of L*, p. 435

26 To Agnes Gertrude Stonehewer Merton [Aunt Kit], 27 May 1964, *R to J*, p. 63

27 To Father Aelred SSF, 8 December 1964, *S of C*, p. 254

28 To Sergius Bolshakoff, 8 December 1965, *HG of L*, p. 106

29 To Sister N., 10 December 1967, *S of C*, p. 355

30 To Agnes Gertrude Stonehewer Merton [Aunt Kit], 27 May 1964, *R to J*, p. 63

DECEMBER

1 Circular letter to friends Advent-Christmas 1967, *R to J*, p.107

2 To Zalman Schachter 15 December 1961, *HG of L*, p. 534

3 To Agnes Gertrude Stonehewer Merton [Aunt Kit], 1 December 1963, *R to J*, p. 60

4 To Zalman Schachter, 15 December 1961, *HG of L*, p. 534

5 To Dorothy Day, 20 December 1961, *HG of L*, p. 141

6 To Sister N., 10 December 1967, *S of C*, p. 355

7 To Dorothy Day, 20 December 1961, *HG of L*, p. 141

8 To Bruno Paul Schlesinger, 13 December 1961, *HG of L*, p. 541

9 To Bruno Paul Schlesinger, 13 December 1961, *HG of L*, p. 543

10 To E.I. Watkin, 12 December 1963, *HG of L*, p. 585

11 To Boris Pasternak, 15 December 1958, *C for T*, p. 92

12 To Dorothy Day, 20 December 1961, *HG of L*, p. 141

13 To Naomi Burton Stone, 29 December 1956, *W to F*, p. 140

14 To Sergius Bolshakoff, 28 December 1962, *HG of L*, p. 103

15 To Zalman Schachter, 15 December 1961, *HG of L*, p. 534

16 To Jeanne Burdick, 26 December 1961, *HG of L*, p. 109

17 To M. S. (Maynard Shelly editor of *The Mennonite*), December 1961, *W to F*, p. 23

18 To Jeanne Burdick, 26 December 1961, *HG of L*, p. 109

19 To Dorothy Day, 20 December 1961, *HG of L*, p. 142
20 To Freida [Nanny} Hauck, 28 December 1964, *R to J*, p. 67
21 To Boris Pasternak, 15 December 1958, *C for T*, p. 92
22 To Dame B., 30 January 1966, *S of C*, p. 297
23 Circular letter to friends, Advent–Christmas 1967, *R to J*, p. 108
24 To Boris Pasternak, 15 December 1958, *C for T*, p. 93
25 To John C. H. Wu, 20 December 1962, *HG of L*, p. 624
26 To Abdul Aziz, 26 December 1962, *HG of L*, p. 53
27 To Sister Elaine M. Bane, 24 December 1965, *S of C*, p. 296
28 To Sister Elaine M. Bane, 24 December 1965, *S of C*, p. 297
29 To Freida [Nanny] Hauck, 22 December 1960, *R to J*, p. 58
30 To John C. H. Wu, 12 December 1961, *HG of L*, p. 621
31 To Sister Anita (Ann) Wasserman OCD, 30 April 1957, *W to F*, p. 185